EMORY AS PLACE

A publication of the
Stuart A. Rose Manuscript,
Archives, and Rare Book Library
at Emory University

EMORY
UNIVERSITY

SERIES EDITOR
Pellom McDaniels III
Emory University

Emory as Place

MEANING IN A UNIVERSITY LANDSCAPE

Gary S. Hauk

with a foreword by Claire E. Sterk

To Jordan Bailey,
with best wishes —

Gary Hauk

The University of Georgia Press   ATHENS

Published by the University of Georgia Press
Athens, Georgia 30602
www.ugapress.org
© 2019 by Emory University
All rights reserved

Designed by Erin Kirk New
Set in Minion Pro and Whitney
Printed and bound by Versa Press, Inc.
The paper in this book meets the guidelines for
permanence and durability of the Committee on
Production Guidelines for Book Longevity of the
Council on Library Resources.

Most University of Georgia Press titles are
available from popular e-book vendors.

Printed in the United States of America
23   22   21   20   19   C   5   4   3   2   1

Library of Congress Cataloging-in-Publication Data

Names: Hauk, Gary S., author.
Title: Emory as place : meaning in a university landscape
    / by Gary S. Hauk ; with a foreword by Claire E. Sterk.
Description: Athens : The University of Georgia Press,
    2019. | Includes bibliographical references and index.
Identifiers: LCCN 2018057930 | ISBN 9780820355627
    (hardcover : alk. paper)
Subjects: LCSH: Emory University—History. | Emory
    University—Buildings. | Universities and colleges—
    Landscape architecture—Georgia—Atlanta.
Classification: LCC LD1751.E382 H38 2019 | DDC
    378.009758/231—dc23

LC record available at https://lccn.loc.gov/2018057930

"A place belongs forever to whoever claims it hardest, remembers it

most obsessively, wrenches it from itself, shapes it, renders it,

loves it so radically that he remakes it in his own image."

—Joan Didion, *The White Album*

"There is something palpable about the landscape of Emory,

the buildings, the trees, and so forth that you never forget,

and anyone who has been a student or staff member or faculty

member at Emory will know what I mean."

—William B. Dillingham 1955C 1956G, Charles Howard Candler

Professor of English, Emeritus

Contents

Foreword

THOSE OF US who work in higher education spend much of our time planning for the future. Faculty and staff, alumni and trustees—nearly all of us, at one time or another, find ourselves involved in strategic priority setting.

These exercises have their benefits. Strategic planning helps us envision what our institutions can become and prompts us to set measurable goals for achieving that vision. Thinking about what lies ahead empowers us to strive for excellence and to work with greater energy and precision. It also ensures that we stay focused on our larger mission.

Yet universities are more than engines propelling us into a bold new future. They are also living history. A college campus serves as a repository for the memories of countless students, staff, and faculty who have passed through its halls. The history of a university resides not just in its archives but also in the place itself—in the walkways and bridges, in the libraries and classrooms, in the gardens and creeks winding their way across campus. This history is alive, and it is also silent. It exists right outside our windows.

I first met Gary Hauk in the late 1990s, when I was a faculty member in the Rollins School of Public Health and Gary was vice president and secretary of Emory University. I was serving as one of the cochairs of the Commission on Research at Emory and needed to give a presentation to the board of trustees on our commission's findings. Gary and I met to discuss the presentation and place it on the board's agenda.

I remember being immediately impressed with his understanding of Emory's past. I also remember his remarkable eye for historical detail. Gary knew the story *behind* the story of Emory. He helped me see that Emory's students, faculty, and staff are the recipients of an extraordinary institutional inheritance, a historical treasure trove that requires us to be thoughtful and dedicated stewards for the sake of our shared future.

In the years since we first connected, my respect for Gary and his scholarship has only deepened. And I believe the book you are about to read represents his most significant contribution to date.

Emory as Place retrieves Emory's physical, architectural, and environmental history, showing us, in Gary's words, "how landscape creates meaning." It offers a series of meticulously researched meditations on sites across our campus. From Seney Hall to Hardman Cemetery, from the building of the Woodruff Health Sciences Center Administration Building to the controversial construction of the road through Lullwater Preserve, Gary touches on all of Emory's landmarks, visible and no longer visible. And at the center of everything lies the Quad—that great space for gathering, for dissent, protest, mourning, and, of course, celebration and commencement.

But this book is more than a reminder of Emory's physical past. Gary has also implicated *us*, his readers, in these pages. Any honest history of Emory University must address the complicated dimensions of our institutional legacy. Gary reminds us that memory, repentance, and grace are entwined. The act of remembering has an ethical dimension; *to remember* requires acknowledging injustice, that is, requires stepping into a given reality and naming it for what it was or is.

Gary describes, for example, the powerful personal experience he had meeting a great-grandson of former Emory president (and white Methodist bishop) George Foster Pierce and discovering that this great-grandson was of African American heritage—a pointed reminder of the subjugation that African American people endured at the hands of the white men, including Pierce, who helped build and lead Emory. That encounter, and Gary's candid reflection on the painful realities of Emory's past, make this book essential reading for all members of today's Emory community. "What do we do with the racist past of an institution that strives to serve humanity?" he asks, and appropriately, he does not provide a pat or quick answer.

Gary's charge to us, his readers, also appears in his account of the oldest living inhabitants of our community: the trees. Newcomers to Emory will find it hard to imagine that our sprawling research complex was once a school nestled in a forest. Gary reminds us that

Emory used to be surrounded by the original Piedmont forest that covered much of the southeastern United States. But growth took its toll on our forest canopy, at Emory and across metropolitan Atlanta and beyond. During the heyday of deforestation, some Emory students earned tuition by chopping down trees. The demand for tree removal grew so high that the university built its own sawmill on campus near what is now the Rita Anne Rollins Building of the Candler School of Theology.

Those days, thankfully, are over, and Emory in recent years has become a global leader in sustainability efforts for college campuses. But that period of our history remains visible to those who look for it. Gary invites us to notice the remaining loblolly pines scattered here and there between our buildings, those "lonely sentinels," he calls them, reminding us of a very different time in our institutional life, a time that has largely vanished.

Gary concludes that in some ways "it is the amazing grace of the trees that keeps the human spirit green." To this thought I would add: it is the amazing dedication of a historian like Gary that keeps the Emory spirit alive. I echo his invitation to his readers: let's engage in the difficult and wonderful work of recollection, both by reading this book and, perhaps even more importantly, by taking a walk around our beautiful campus. One could say that our future depends on it.

Claire E. Sterk
President, Emory University

INTRODUCTION

Genius Loci

SOMETIME IN THE FIRST DECADE of the twenty-first century, it became fashionable among Emory College seniors to try to check off a bucket list before Commencement. The roster of fairly challenging (and sometimes actually dangerous) activities included pulling off illicit pranks without implicating oneself and sneaking into off-limit spaces without triggering alarms. High on the list every year was the old, boarded-up mansion of Asa Candler Jr. that stood rotting atop its foundation on Emory's Briarcliff property: how to get into that? Occasionally seniors would climb the fence surrounding the private pool behind the president's home in Lullwater and take a midnight dip. Often students looked for a way past the locked metal door that led, they had heard, from the boiler plant behind the sorority lodges into the legendary steam tunnels that supposedly spread under the campus like a network of catacombs. (Who knew what creatures lived there?) Once, several students tried to navigate the vertiginous stairs and perilous ladder up to the belfry of Glenn Memorial for the perfect Snapchat photo. Harking back to Emory of an earlier day were those climbers who scrambled by stairs or other means to the top of Seney Hall on the Oxford campus, where they set the bell to clanging in the clock tower—usually at 2:00 or 3:00 a.m.

Never, to my knowledge, did the seniors' bucket list include some of the more arcane possibilities on the Emory campus: finding the unmarked graves of the Methodist bishops who loved Emory so much they asked to be buried under the Quadrangle; passing a night in the Tufts House, where someone once spotted the ghost of a woman in search of her dead son; spending a night in the

1

cemetery on Clairmont Campus, where the wind might carry the moans of the spirits of Union soldiers who died in the chapel that once stood there; or circumnavigating the Atlanta campus by following the streams that flow into each other along the campus perimeter.

True—those bishops' graves never (I think) existed. And the woman encountered by the computing center staff member one night in 1971 may or may not have been truly ghostly. Those soldiers' groans may be only the imagination at play, and the journey by stream around the campus requires almost as much undaunted courage as the Lewis and Clark expedition. Still, all of these possibilities, like those on the students' bucket list, suggest something important. These actual or possible interactions with the landscape and the buildings suggest that the campus and its environs exert an influence on people. The university as a physical entity—quite apart from its conceptual existence as "a seat of learning" or "a higher education institution"—has a kind of personality and being that people can engage with. In fact, one could go so far as to say that it has what the ancient Romans called *genius loci*—the genius or quality or character specific to the place.

For the ancients, the genius of a place was its guardian spirit, the power that protected and watched over it, the resident feeling of holiness that inspired or infused anything mortals might do there. For us moderns, the term may suggest more the atmosphere of the place—its look and feel, but also its breath and heartbeat and energy. The genius or character of the place resides in the blend of aesthetics and ethos that the place evokes the moment we step into it. A cathedral differs in this respect from a shopping mall, and the genius loci of Gettysburg varies quite a bit from that of Ellis Island, even as both evoke unique histories that in some ways define America.

To think of a university as a place in this sense is to think of it as more than a locus of study, more than a destination for scholars, and even more than a campus. A campus, after all, was for the Romans nothing more than a field. Even "the campus" at Princeton, where the word was first applied in a collegiate context, simply marked the vacant acres separating the main college building, Nassau Hall, from the high street of the town.[1]

To think of Emory as place, as this book invites you to do, is to consider its geography and its architecture—the lay of the land and the built-up spaces its people inhabit. It is also to imagine how the external, constructed world leads to an internal world of wonder and purpose and responsibility—in short, how a landscape creates meaning. Emory as place offers physical, though mute, evidence of how landscape and population have shaped each other over decades of debate about architecture, curriculum, and resources. More than that, the physical development of the place mirrors the university's awareness of itself as an arena of tension between the past and the future—even between the past and the present, between what the university has been and what it now purports or intends to be, through its spaces. Most of all, thinking of Emory as place suggests a way to get at the core meaning of an institution as large, diverse, complex, and tentacled as a modern research university. An illustration or two may be in order.

Emory College was founded in a small town by devout Methodists who viewed the classical liberal arts curriculum as the key to forming responsible and morally upright white, male citizens for a still young American republic. Emory University exists today as a high-level research institution with a liberal arts college, professional schools, a vast health sciences enterprise, expensive but productive global connections, and a campus population as diverse as any in the United States in terms of racial, gender, geographical, and socioeconomic origins. How are these two—the little college in the small town, and the university in the big city—the same institution? In what sense can anyone say that the original campus, in Oxford, Georgia, bears any genetic connection to the newer campus forty miles away, in Atlanta, the busiest capital of the southeastern United States? It is as if—in an example offered by Marshall Duke, a distinguished psychology professor at Emory—someone had bought a car in 1960 and, over the next fifty years, replaced nearly every part. In what sense is it the same car?[2]

I would push Marshall's analogy further: it is as if someone bought a Chevrolet roadster in 1915 and spent the next century adding bells and whistles and all the accoutrements of a twenty-first-century vehicle—seatbelts, airbags, a catalytic converter, fuel injection, ABS brakes—to create a car suitable for the interstate. It's a quite different automobile, but somehow the old Chevy is still there. If Marshall will forgive my borrowing his example, maybe he will forgive me for adding the suggestion that the Haygood-Hopkins Gate at the entrance to Emory's Atlanta campus may be the hood ornament of that car. The gate was erected in 1937, just a little over two decades after the Druid Hills campus in Atlanta was opened. The gate honors the memory of two great Emory presidents of the nineteenth century, Atticus Greene Haygood and Isaac Stiles Hopkins. The alumnus who paid for the gate, Linton Robeson 1886C, graduated after spending his first two years at Emory College during Haygood's presidency and his last two during that of Hopkins.[3]

More than memorializing these two great men, however, the gate stands as a reminder of that original campus forty miles away. It recalls the humble origins of the college and the struggles to survive. Importantly, it recalls the values of the institution—values not always lived out perfectly but often articulated as a goal. Haygood voiced the hope for a new day in the South when racial and sectional reconciliation would be possible; Hopkins embodied the aspiration for a modern, industrial economy that would lift the South out of its poverty and provincialism. Both men had grown up in a society dependent on the enslavement of a large part of the population but had found ample reason to be grateful for the demise of that society.

Thus, the move of the college from Oxford forced the institution to wrestle with what its past meant—not only the nostalgia of generations of students who had gone to school at Oxford but also Emory's entwinement with the antebellum institution of slavery. The gate is in some ways the first instance of how the geography and the built environment of the Atlanta campus would come to reflect the institution's willingness to look at its mistakes and to strive for improvement. In the words of Haygood chiseled into the left pillar of the gate, "Let us stand by what is good and try to make it better"—with the implication of leaving behind what is narrow, inhumane, and untrue.

Here is another example. Cannon Chapel, consecrated in 1981, serves as a teaching and worship space for Emory's Candler School of Theology, one of the two largest United Methodist seminaries in the world (the other is Duke Divinity School, which regularly trades first and second places with Candler). The chapel, bearing the name of William Ragsdale Cannon, a former dean of Candler and later a bishop of the United Methodist Church, is a token of Emory's Methodist heritage. At the same time, Cannon

Chapel serves every religious community on campus: on Friday afternoons, Muslims gather in the sanctuary for prayers; Jews use the same space for services on high holy days; Buddhists meditate there on Monday evenings; and Sunday mornings find Protestants gathering for an ecumenical worship service after the Roman Catholic Mass. The chapel thus stands as a symbol of Emory's long institutional engagement with religious life and with the moral purposes of higher education that transcend religious boundaries. In the words of the preamble to the university's original bylaws, Emory "is designed to be a profoundly religious institution without being narrowly sectarian. It proposes to encourage freedom of thought as liberal as the limitations of truth."

Emory makes itself vulnerable to charges of presumption or hypocrisy by declaring in its vision statement that it is "ethically engaged."[4] Yet that commitment links the small college with the research university, as Emory has retooled ethics and religion from the university's Methodist roots to address the global concerns shared by all faiths. Cannon Chapel was the site of President Bill Clinton's Southern Regional Economic Conference in 1995 and the venue where the Dalai Lama joined Emory president William M. Chace in signing a partnership agreement between the university and Tibetan Buddhist institutions in 1998. The chapel also provided a flashpoint over the issue of same-sex commitment ceremonies in the 1990s and is thus a reminder of how Emory has sought (not always successfully) to adapt to new realities while balancing tradition and change. In a sense—returning to Marshall's illustration of the car remade over decades—Cannon Chapel symbolizes the engine of aspiration that propels the university, an engine that now uses hybrid technology (multifaith perspectives) to meet the needs of a different environment.

Any university campus serves, on the one hand, as the scene of the mysterious ignition of artistic and scholarly creativity and, on the other hand, as the setting for the simple quotidian activities of eating and walking. The campus marries local history to the possibilities of the future. In Emory's case, this means association with the legacies and potential of the financial and cultural capital of the Southeast. The hardscape of historic buildings and walkways as well as the landscape of groves, gardens, and greenery not only reward the backward glance of custom, memory, and tradition but also foster the forward gaze of thought, hope, and imagination. In this sense, the university is a habitation where, to paraphrase Alexis de Tocqueville, habits of mind and heart take root. It is a space for developing discipline for a certain kind of life—a life of exploration far beyond the campus gate. As a place, then, Emory is a home for the spirit and mind and body. Those who have inhabited it will continue to dwell there for years to come, because alma mater inhabits them.

Yet for those who have experienced Emory for any extended time, habit is often challenged by change: the place remembered never stays the same. The hill of grass that used to slope down toward the street at the western edge of the campus gave way years ago to a parking lot and later to a building. The college in the forest has morphed into an urban scene where trees have left "the woods" to become part of a "streetscape." For those who have lived in the place longer than usual—for decades, perhaps, rather than a few years of study—the university seems to have experienced every bit as much change as their own aging bodies. Time brings both blessing and loss to universities as well as persons—new gifts for which to give thanks but also familiar objects or ways to which we sometimes must bid farewell.

In more recent years, faculty members and administrators have sought ways to encourage Emory students to complete a different sort of bucket list—enjoying at least one concert or recital every year in the Schwartz Center for Performing Arts; volunteering every semester at some opportunity for community service somewhere in Atlanta; inviting at least one faculty member to lunch or coffee for conversation; attending a performance of Theater Emory; cheering on an athletic team; participating in homecoming activities; dancing at Dooley's Ball. While the aim of such a list always has been to broaden students' experience, introduce them to the diverse university and metropolitan communities, and deepen the education of their hearts as well as their minds, the end is always an enrichment of their sense of the university as a place where, for a short time, they dwell.

This book pays homage to the spirit of the place called Emory through archival photos that correct or reinforce memory. Captions connect the place that was to the place that now is, but they also suggest the distinctive constant change of the place. Along the way, brief personal essays seek to fill the nooks and crannies where what used to be has fallen out of view. Though people have come and gone, though buildings have risen and fallen, and though the world has come to Emory in new and surprising ways, through it all, the place called Emory continues to breathe a certain, distinctive spirit that is its genius.

CHAPTER 1

Oxford   *The Mother Campus*

EMORY COLLEGE grew from a seedling planted in 1834, two years before the founding of the college. That year, members of the Georgia Conference of the Methodist Episcopal Church took note of an educational fad that had begun in Germany, and they established what they called the Georgia Conference Manual Labor School, just west of Covington. Students pursuing a college-preparatory course would take classes and study in the morning, then work in fields or at mechanical trades for several hours in the afternoon to help offset the cost of their education and learn the discipline of practical work. Following "tea" and later supper, the students would return to their studies in the evening.[1]

Successful at first, the school soon veered toward bankruptcy. (The logic of the plan may have been canceled by a certain illogic, as teachers and students did not always make good farmers.) Undaunted by the prospect of a failed prep school, the trustees and Georgia Methodists decided to set their sights higher and established a college called Emory. Receiving its charter on December 10, 1836, the college honored the memory of Methodist bishop John Emory of Maryland, who had died the year before in a carriage accident, but not before leaving a legacy of commitment to education at Wesleyan University and Dickinson College.

The early curriculum at Emory, as at most liberal-arts colleges in the nineteenth century, heavily emphasized the classical trivium—grammar, logic, and rhetoric—and the extracurricular activities of two literary societies augmented students' striving in these subjects, if not always their perfect achievement. From its earliest days, Emory College has been home to debate, represented by the buildings made possible by these literary societies. Phi Gamma

The building shown here was one of several two-room structures that served the Manual Labor School on its four hundred acres west of Covington. A historical marker in the Clark's Grove section of Covington, about half a mile west of the town square, tells some of the history. When the school's trustees closed the foundering school in 1840, Emory College assumed its assets and liabilities and moved this building to the new campus in Oxford. The building has long since gone into the same oblivion as the Manual Labor School.

Ironically, in 2011 an alumnus donated eleven acres to Oxford College just seven hundred feet from the campus for the purpose of developing an organic farm, which has been in operation as a teaching and research environment since 2014 while also providing food for the college dining hall. The place and the curriculum in some respects came full circle.

Hall, the oldest academic building owned by Emory, was built in 1851 by members of the college's first literary society, who raised the funds for their impressive clubhouse. The society was formed in 1837 by Manual Labor School students who would become the first students of Emory College the next year. (Phi and gamma are the Greek initials of the society's name, *Philos tes Gnoses*—friend or lover of knowledge.) A kind of fraternity, Phi Gamma was also a debate team, a book club, and an eating society—the hub of social life on the remote and tiny college campus.

As often happens in human communities, one society or in-group prompted the birth of a rival group, and in 1839 students on the outside of Phi Gamma created a rival literary society named

Phi Gamma Hall.

At Commencement in 1951, Phi Gamma alumni re-created the old-time debates. On the podium are, left to right, Professor Henry M. Quillian 1913C, Dr. Paul E. Bryan 1907C, Charles E. Middlebrooks Jr., and Dr. O. O. Fanning 1907C.

for Ignatius Alphonso Few, the first president of Emory. Sometimes denoted with the Greek letters phi epsilon upsilon to spell "FEU," the Few Society built its own hall on the northeast corner of the campus, facing Phi Gamma. The date of construction is uncertain but may have been as early as 1848, according to Oxford historian Erik Oliver, making Few, not Phi Gamma, the oldest academic building owned by Emory.[2] These buildings also housed the first real libraries of Emory, as the literary societies developed their own collections independently of the college. (Early Emory historian Henry Morton Bullock estimates that in 1860, the societies together owned about 4,000 volumes, compared to the college's 1,900.)[3] Both Phi Gamma Hall and Few Hall were used as hospitals to care for wounded soldiers after the Battle of Atlanta in 1864.

Well after the college moved to Atlanta in 1919, the two literary societies continued to serve as a focal point for student life and refined the rhetorical talents of Emory graduates. The societies' legacy lives on in the Barkley Forum, Emory's nationally renowned debate program.

When Emory College welcomed its first students for classes in September 1838, the "campus plant," as we would now call it, comprised four two-story brick buildings for instruction, a wooden steward's hall, and a wooden chapel, all spread in a row along the southern edge of the campus (the lower border of the "College Square" in the town plan on page 45). None of those buildings endured.

In 1852, the college erected Old Main on the site now occupied by Seney Hall. The weight of the tower on Old Main proved too great for the supporting walls, which began to collapse, and the college razed the building in 1872. Less than a decade after war had touched the campus, the loss of this main building may have made the place feel very impermanent.

Legend says that the five-hundred-pound bell originally housed in Old Main, and now installed in the tower of Seney Hall, was a gift from Queen Victoria to Emory's fourth president, the scientist Alexander Means, during a visit to England in the mid-1850s. Its actual provenance remains a mystery. The same legend recounts that President Means was made an honorary member of the Royal Society during that English sojourn, although the Royal Society has no record of Means's presence.[4] Perhaps associating their president with the British queen was a way for the collegians to elevate their stature in their own minds.

Although the college originally had built four small residence halls for students, many students lived in the town. In 1855, President Means called the residence halls "facilities for mischief" and recommended that the board of trustees close the halls and require all students to live off campus; the board declined. Four years later, President James R. Thomas repeated the recommendation, and this time the board concurred. Thus, during the decades following the Civil War, through the first decade of the twentieth century, students at Emory College boarded with families in the town of Oxford.

A brief, unsigned history of Emory in the university archives recalls the shaping influence on students of living in the homes of administrators, teachers, and even presidents of the college. The unnamed author attributes much of "the intangible Oxford spirit" to the loving care the "boys" received in the homes of the townspeople, some of them with as many as six or seven boarders.

In this photo, the class of 1860 poses with Old Main in the background. The obelisk in the center is the Few Monument, erected in 1849 in memory of the college's first president, three years after his death. The bell shown at the top of the cornice of Old Main survived to clang forth while suspended from a post or tree branch near the chapel until the construction of Seney Hall, from whose tower the bell now rings.

Just where the students in this photo are lounging is uncertain. The back of the
photo calls the house Orna Villa, which was the first house built in Newton County
(1825) and was for many years the home of President Alexander Means. The front,
however, bears little resemblance to that of Orna Villa today but does share the
same decorative iron work as the President's House (circa 1836) and the home
of Professor George W. W. Stone (1837 or 1838). Whichever house it was, it may
have boarded students when this photo was taken, sometime around 1900.
The photo back identifies the students as members of Sigma Alpha Epsilon,
one of the first fraternities sanctioned by Emory College after the Civil War.

Customarily, families and students often gathered after the evening meal for songs and prayers in the parlor, and then the students would linger for conversation into the night.[5]

Original Haygood Hall.

Some students felt keenly the expense of boarding: M. B. Summerlin, writing to his father in 1851, complained, "Expenses are so much, boarding and lodging is twelve Dollars per month exclusive of washing, wood, and lights . . . Tuition is $50 a year. This is an extravagant place."[6]

To ease the cost of living, President Haygood received permission from the trustees for students to live in "helping halls"—essentially self-managed co-ops in which the students prepared their own meals and maintained their own space.

The Oxford campus would not have another residence hall until 1913, when Haygood Hall became the first dormitory on the campus since those rude brick structures built in 1838 had been torn down before the Civil War. When the first women enrolled at Oxford as residential students in 1954, the college assigned them to D wing, which quickly became dubbed the Doll House. After fire destroyed Haygood Hall in 1981, Oxford College rebuilt it on a slightly smaller scale and continues to house students there.

When the Civil War erupted in 1861, Emory trustees closed the college in November of that year in hope that hostilities soon would be over, and that the students who had gone off to war would return to fill the classrooms. More than four years passed before President Thomas and two other faculty members—Luther M. Smith and George W. W. Stone—courageously reopened the campus in January 1866. The buildings, damaged by war and by use as military hospitals, needed significant repair, equipment and materials needed to be replaced, and the faculty had to get by on reduced salaries. (Stone helped support his colleague with produce from his nearby farms.)[7]

The demolition of Old Main in 1872 left only Phi Gamma and Few as campus buildings that offered both a connection to the earliest days of the college and a sense that the college would continue to have a future. Everything else was vulnerable to weather and rot. A capital campaign led by Bishop George Foster Pierce, who had served as the third president of Emory (1848–1854), raised enough money to build Language Hall and three other buildings—Science Hall (now Humanities Hall), the Chapel, and a recitation hall, now gone, near where Seney Hall now stands. Completed in 1874, Language Hall would gain a neighbor to its west with the completion of Seney Hall in 1881. An extensive renovation completed in 2012 brought Language Hall up to ADA standards while restoring exterior details of the original design.

The Chapel can seat about 180. Here, until 1919, Emory College students attended mandatory chapel services twice a day (the faculty had to attend only once daily) and heard announcements from the president and sermons and inspirational talks from the faculty or visiting dignitaries. As the college catalog of 1904–1905 put it, "the authorities" of the college were unwilling to remove students "from the influences and restraints of home at a period of life when passion is strongest and habits are forming, without bringing to bear the most direct and intentional effort to secure their religious well-being." While the chapel services were nonsectarian, "a pronounced Christian life is urged upon all students."[8]

Here, too, students occasionally played pranks, as when someone suspended the skeleton from the science lab over the pulpit on a morning when President James E. Dickey was scheduled to preach. (That skeleton became known as Dooley, who still appears regularly on campus as the unofficial embodiment of the "spirit of Emory.")[9]

Language Hall.

Oxford Chapel.

This undated photo of a
crowd gathered at the Oxford
chapel may show activities
during the 1936 centennial of
Emory College.

Atticus Greene Haygood
1859c (1839–1896).

President Atticus Greene Haygood is seated third from left in this 1877 photo. With him are, left to right seated, Luther M. Smith 1848c, George W. W. Stone Sr. 1842c, Haygood, Alexander Means, Henry A. Scomp, and Morgan Callaway; standing are Rigdon M. McIntosh and John Fletcher Bonnell 1871c. Stone taught at Emory from 1843 until his death in 1889, with interruptions to teach at Wesleyan College and to sit out the Civil War. McIntosh achieved immortality as the arranger of the best-known version of the gospel hymn "Bound for the Promised Land." Bonnell taught from 1875 until Emory College moved to Atlanta in 1919, a forty-four-year record of service not surpassed until the twenty-first century.

After Emory College moved to Atlanta in 1919, the Chapel continued in use for religious services. By the 1950s, the Chapel had become overgrown with vines and shrubbery, and the university contemplated razing it. Fortunately, a campaign to refurbish the building led to its reclamation as a historic and still-usable structure. Aiming to create a more adaptable space for various uses in the twenty-first century, the administration replaced the Chapel's undistinguished old pews with comfortable chairs that could be rearranged for concerts, seminars, and retreats as well as worship—or stacked and moved completely out of the way altogether for yoga on the floor.

A decade after the end of the Civil War, as the old campus gained new life with new structures, it also received a shot in the

arm from a new president. Atticus Greene Haygood 1859C became president in 1875 and served until 1884. He gained fame for himself and the college when he preached his famous "New South" sermon in November 1880 in Old Church. In that sermon, he gave thanks for the end of war and slavery, exhorted his fellow southerners to give up pining for the past and to begin building to the future, and offered "new light" on the possibilities of harmony between the races and between North and South. Subtitled "Gratitude, Amendment, Hope," the future-oriented and progress-minded sermon was published at the request of the faculty and found its way into the hands of Brooklyn banker and railroad magnate George I. Seney. Reportedly a descendant of Ignatius Few, the first president of Emory, Seney also hoped to build a railroad in Georgia. A Methodist himself, and perhaps spurred by the thought that Methodists ran much of the state and might aid his railroad enterprise, he made generous contributions to two of Georgia's Methodist colleges—Emory and Wesleyan College in Macon.

Completed in 1881, at a cost of $50,000, the building named for George Seney originally housed the college library as well as offices and classrooms.[10] Seney Hall was also home to the first telegraph installed at Emory. In 1915 the trustees approved the new technology, "provided it was found that it would not injure the building or affect the insurance and was not in conflict with any Federal statute."[11] Seven decades later, the building would be wired for the internet—although board minutes do not record whether trustees debated this latest intrusion of technology.

In 1971, ninety years old, Seney Hall faced demolition. Windows were falling out, plaster ceilings were crumbling, and some slates on the deteriorating roof hung by a single rusty nail. In distant Atlanta, similarly old buildings were giving way to the future: the 1885 Kimball House Hotel came down in 1959 to make way for a parking deck, and the 1905 Beaux Arts Terminal Station was razed in 1972, replaced by the Richard B. Russell Federal Building.[12] Nearly deciding to raze historic Seney Hall, the university instead laid claim to the building's heritage and renovated it from 1976 to 1978 at a cost approaching the then-exorbitant sum of $1 million.

President Haygood resigned in 1884 to take up work as the chief agent of the John F. Slater Fund, supporting educational institutions for African Americans in the South. (He would later become a bishop of the Methodist Episcopal Church, South.) His successor at Emory was classmate Isaac Stiles Hopkins 1859C.

OPPOSITE: Seney Hall. The building appears here in the late 1930s or early 1940s, with Language Hall in the background.

Isaac Stiles Hopkins 1859c (1841–1914).

To teach at Emory College in the nineteenth century required polymathic intelligence, or at least the ability to absorb and then convey new knowledge quickly, and Hopkins was a true master of many disciplines. Like Haygood and every other nineteenth-century Emory president, he was a Methodist minister, but he did not teach religion. He taught natural science, Latin, English literature, "moral science" (ethics), "mental science" (psychology), and—in a pioneering development that would catch the attention of state leaders—"tool craft and design," later called tool craft and technology.

Like Haygood, Hopkins believed that future prosperity for the South would require diversifying the economy beyond agriculture and increasing the region's capacity for manufacturing and industry. To achieve this would take leaders who knew something about machinery. An amateur machinist, he began teaching students in his workshop behind his home in

Hopkins Hall, 1936. The historic structure—putatively the birthplace of Georgia Tech—appears here behind the class of 1886, which gathered for its fiftieth reunion during the college centennial in 1936. One member of this class, Linton Robeson, later gave the funds to build the Haygood-Hopkins Gate at the entrance to the Atlanta campus to memorialize the two men who had presided over Emory during his student years.

Built in 1836 for Ignatius Alphonso Few, who was the first Emory College president and one of the first residents of the new town of Oxford, the President's House, as it came to be called, also became the home of Few's successors, Augustus Baldwin Longstreet and George Foster Pierce. The house served as the home of other citizens of the town before Atticus Haygood purchased it in the first year of his Emory presidency, 1875. In 1889, trustee Young L. G. Harris bought the house and presented it to the college. Since then, the house has been the official home of Emory presidents and, after the move of Emory College to Atlanta, the home of Oxford College deans.

The original house had a dining room and parlor on opposite sides of a central hallway downstairs, with two bedrooms on the second floor. President Longstreet added wings to the front, and at some point an extension was added to the back. In desperate need of repair by 2005, the historic building underwent extensive renovation, including abatement of lead paint, rebuilding of the porches, salvaging and remilling of the heart-pine floorboards, and sealing of the house to protect it from water penetration (Jacobs, "Oxford College President's House Gets a New Lease on Life"). This photo from 1974 shows Dean Bond Fleming between two ancient magnolias that were later cut down to open a view to the front of the house.

23

A side view of the President's House, 1974.

Oxford and in 1884, with President Haygood's blessing, introduced a "school of tool craft and design" into the curriculum. As president of the college (1884–1888), Hopkins persuaded the trustees to erect a new building to house this innovative effort. Hopkins Hall served as the home of technological education at Emory until the state of Georgia caught on and recruited Hopkins away to become the first president of the Georgia Institute of Technology (Georgia Tech)—arguably the second great research institution founded at Oxford, after Emory. With the departure of Hopkins, the technological focus at Emory waned, and the building became home to a gymnasium and, later, a swimming pool. Hopkins Hall now serves as the home of the Eady Admissions Center of Oxford College.

The departure of Hopkins for Georgia Tech opened the door for one of the more remarkable graduates of Emory to assume the presidency and begin a four-decade devotion to reshaping the institution. Graduating from Emory College in 1875, Warren Akin Candler left many legacies to Emory from his decade as president of the college (1888–1898) and his five years as the first chancellor of the university (1915–1920). Candler raised academic standards and modernized the curriculum, introducing a department of theology and strengthening the study of law begun during the Haygood years, while phasing out vocational programs in bookkeeping and telegraphy.[13] Importantly, he brought his older brother Asa Griggs Candler Sr., founder of the Coca-Cola Company, onto the Emory board of trustees. Together, the two of them would help to change Emory history by engineering the creation of a new university in Atlanta and the merger of Emory College with the university.

Notoriously, President Candler encouraged the trustees to establish a long-standing policy prohibiting intercollege athletics. (This was at a time when great traditions in football and basketball were taking root across the country—a period that bypassed Emory. Intercollegiate sports, while permitted on a very small scale at the Atlanta campus, would not become a significant student activity at Emory until the university helped establish the University Athletic Association in 1986.)[14] Candler called intercollegiate sports "evil, wholly evil, and that always." He believed—and who can argue—that intercollegiate sports diverted students' attention from the aims of learning, wasted institutional resources that should otherwise be spent on academics, and tempted people to gambling. Nevertheless, he had a healthy appreciation for the ancient ideal of *mens sana in corpore sano* (a healthy mind in a healthy body).

Thus, while Emory is infamous as a major southern university that has never fielded an intercollegiate football team, the university has a long and storied history of athletic excellence. In 1897 Candler hired Frank Clyde Brown from the Cumberland, Maryland, YMCA to create one of the first organized intramural programs among American colleges. (Coach Brown doubled as the professor of Romance languages and later professor of English—an unusual combination of coaching and faculty responsibilities unlikely to be found on most college campuses today.) Candler authorized the purchase of a field near the campus for athletics and had Hopkins Hall converted into a gymnasium. By the first decade of the new century, the administration and trustees recognized the need for a more modern, larger recreational facility. Trustee Jesse Williams made the lead gift toward the project.

By the time the new gymnasium opened in 1907, the building and its equipment cost nearly twenty-eight

Warren Akin Candler (1857–1941).

Asa Griggs Candler Sr.
(1851–1929).

Warren Candler is the sun around whom the faculty orbit in this photo from 1893. James E. Dickey 1891c, in the upper left, would go on to become the last president of Emory before the college moved to Atlanta. Harry Harlan Stone 1880c, who appears to be looking at Candler's forehead, was the son of George W. W. Stone Sr. 1842c. George Sr. spent most of his life at Emory, and Harry outdid him, living all his life at Oxford and serving as a faculty member, librarian, and treasurer of the college, as well as designer of the original seal of the university. Too attached to the town of Oxford and the old campus that had harbored him, Harry Stone declined to move to Atlanta with the college in 1919 and concluded his career teaching in the Emory Academy, a preparatory school the university operated on the old campus for about a decade and a half after the college moved.

thousand dollars, more than ten thousand dollars over its projected budget, but was considered by the trustees to be the best gymnasium in the South and one that would "meet the needs of the institution for half a century or more."[15] The arrival of women as residential students in 1954 made locker rooms necessary for them, and the university responded by building an addition to the back of the gymnasium in the 1970s. Further renovation in 2001 created a 180-seat dance studio as part of a larger project to enhance space for performing arts on the Oxford campus.

Williams Gymnasium.

In Warren Candler's last year as president of the college, he led the campaign to raise funds for the first freestanding library at Emory. Before this effort, the library resources of the college had been scattered in Phi Gamma, Few, and Seney Halls. Built in 1898, the new library was named Candler Hall despite the departing president's humble protests.

Candler Hall made for a cozy library, with stacks arranged on the second-floor mezzanine in a kind of pinwheel. In 1971, after the construction of the Hoke O'Kelley Library (renovated and enlarged as the Oxford Library Center in 2014), Oxford College transformed the interior of Candler Hall into the Card Student Center, named for Janice Card 1969ox 1971c, whose father contributed half the funds to renovate the building. An air of venerable quiet still fills the interior when the snack bar is empty.

Pierce Hall cornerstone ceremony. Before being elected a bishop of the Methodist Episcopal Church, South, in 1854, George Foster Pierce (1811–1884) served as the founding president of Wesleyan College and then as the third president of Emory. His wide influence in the church helped raise money for four new buildings on the Emory campus in 1874–1875. (See pages 36–37 for the story of Pierce's African American descendants.) To honor Bishop Pierce's memory, the trustees named a new science building for him.

This rare photograph shows men and women, both white and African American, at the laying of the cornerstone in 1903, during the period of Jim Crow laws in the South. The smiling images in a photo like this probably belie the reality for many residents of the town of Oxford. (Although African American citizens of Oxford were employed by the college, they could not legally enroll as students until 1962, and the first did not enroll until 1968.)

When completed in 1904, Pierce Hall ushered in a new era of luxury as the first building on campus to have steam heat, gas, and running water. By the middle of the century, however, the building had aged poorly; the university razed it and built a new Pierce Hall between Few Hall and Humanities Hall. Dormitories filled the space left by the demolition of the original Pierce Hall. The second Pierce Hall, opened in 1962 and replaced by a new science building in 2016, underwent a renovation completed in 2018 and is now used as a classroom building.

Pierce Hall, 1940s.

Beginning in 1888, a mule-drawn trolley made the two-mile trip between the Oxford campus and downtown Covington easier. Few businesses operated in Oxford, and the nearby county seat, Covington, was a magnet for students wanting more excitement—such as the Depot Store, where students could "get a Good Smoke or a Cold Drink at our stand" while waiting for the train, or a barber shop that offered "clean linen, sharp razors, polite barbers," and "hot and cold tub and shower baths" (advertisement, *Emory Comet* [1910], Stuart A. Rose Library). The Covington and Oxford Street Railway operated this trolley line until 1917. According to Oxford resident and historian Erik Oliver, the line had a turnaround and a barn near Old Church (Oliver, *Images of America*, 30).

Allen Memorial Church. Among the most famous Emory alumni of the nineteenth century—at least in Methodist circles—was Young John Allen 1858c. In many ways, he exemplified the ideal outcome of the educational program the founders put in place—a graduate deeply imbued with faith, who felt the responsibility (and had the brains) for improving the lot of humanity. A year after his graduation he married, and in 1860 he left with his wife and infant daughter to serve as a missionary to China, where he lived until his death in 1907. Principally a publisher and educator, he translated many works of Chinese into English, as well as English religious tracts into Chinese. His list of publications exceeds 250 books. He founded a school for girls and enlisted Laura Haygood, sister of Emory president Atticus Haygood, to run it. Widely honored during his lifetime, both in China and in the United States, Allen received an honorary degree from Emory in 1878 on one of his sabbatical visits home.

Allen Memorial in Oxford, constructed in 1910 and named for Young John Allen, provided a much-needed modern facility to replace the Old Church, both for regular worship services and for occasional convocations and other assemblies for the college. Owned by Emory University, today it welcomes first-year students for opening convocations and graduating sophomores for baccalaureate services.

On the steps of Candler Hall on June 9, 1914, the trustees of Emory College must have had much on their minds. In March the Tennessee State Supreme Court had ruled against the Methodist Episcopal Church, South, in its lawsuit against Vanderbilt University to determine who had authority over the direction of Vanderbilt. The Emory trustees in June pondered the opportunity arising for Emory College in the new university soon to be born. Bishop Warren Candler is seated third from the left, and his brother Asa Griggs Candler Sr. is seated second from the right.

Nearly eighty years after the founding of Emory College, the Methodist Episcopal Church, South, severed its relationship with Vanderbilt University over a dispute about that university's founding and trusteeship. Determined to establish a new university in the Southeast, the denomination appointed a commission chaired by Warren Candler, now a bishop, to decide where to locate the new university. Atlanta was very much in the running, and the Emory trustees in June 1914 discussed the possibility of merging Emory College with the new university if Atlanta were chosen as the site. The two men who would make it all happen were Bishop Candler and his brother Asa Griggs Candler Sr., who in July 1914 wrote his famous "million-dollar letter" offering the first funds for the enterprise. He would give much more, including the first seventy-five acres for the new campus in the Druid Hills suburb of Atlanta.[16]

The chartering of Emory University in DeKalb County in 1915 set in motion the move of Emory College from Oxford four years later. Sentiment argued for keeping the original campus in the university family. After all, generations of alumni had spent countless hours studying there, had formed enduring friendships, had launched from there into careers of every stripe, and had come to harbor memories of the literal groves of academe that comprised the tree-filled campus and town.

There were also practical reasons for holding on to the Oxford campus, as Emory trustees considered the potential for creating a first-class prep school in the South along the lines of distinguished northeastern academies like Phillips Exeter or the Lawrenceville School. From 1915 until 1929, the Emory University Academy offered a college-preparatory curriculum. Then the university experimented with various ways of combining the last years of high school with the first two years of college in a program designated as Emory-at-Oxford, or EAO, from 1929 to 1964. At last, in 1964, Emory ended the precollege curriculum and established Oxford College of Emory University in its current format, as a two-year college whose graduates may continue automatically to Emory College on the Atlanta campus to complete their undergraduate programs in the liberal arts, business, or nursing. Oxford College is, in American higher education, a unique second doorway into the liberal arts experience of a research university.[17]

The *Emory College Bulletin* published in July 1906 included a multipanel pullout with two panoramic photographs capturing the entire campus as it appeared in the first decade of the twentieth century. In this year a race riot rocked the capital of Georgia and left between twenty-five and forty African Americans and two whites dead, while a continent away, in San Francisco, an earthquake and fire killed some three thousand people and leveled hundreds of city blocks. In bucolic Oxford, the two hundred or so students enrolled that year in the college may have felt just as removed from the hazards of city life as the college founders had intended.

The first panorama, looking south, shows, from the left, a corner of Humanities Hall, Candler Hall, Language Hall, Seney Hall, and Hopkins Hall, with Williams Gymnasium nearing completion and still surrounded by scaffolding.

The second panorama, looking north, shows, left to right, the Chapel, Phi Gamma, the Few Monument in the middle of the green, Pierce Science Hall, Few Hall, and Humanities Hall. In the more than a century since this photo was taken, the "grove of academe" on the green has remained, and newer trees have grown even taller than those shown here. New construction—residence halls, a library, and a science building—has filled the open spaces between buildings to square off the area as a true quadrangle, graced by brick sidewalks and closed to automobile traffic.

CHAPTER 2

Emory's Early Entwinement with Slavery

ONLY AFTERWARD did I come to understand the significance of that moment for Emory—the moment when I came face to face, literally, with the reality of sexual relations between master and enslaved in the antebellum South. While it left me with unanswered questions, it confirmed that the world into which Emory was born, before the Civil War, was one that requires imagination to fathom.

The occasion was a ceremony of celebration and remembrance in the Old Church at Oxford. Emory was marking the end of a six-year examination of the university's racial history and the beginning of still more study toward trying to redeem the past. The day had begun for my wife, Sara, and me at Grace United Methodist Church in Covington, Georgia, a historically black church. There, Emory trustee and Methodist bishop Mike Watson preached a sermon about memory, repentance, and grace near the end of a three-hour service that included a great deal of singing, much testifying, and heartfelt prayers. That afternoon, at Old Church, another long program included recognition of descendants of enslaved African Americans who had lived in Oxford and a statement of regret from the Emory board of trustees read by the Emory president, James W. Wagner.

As the afternoon program concluded, and the audience rose to stretch and begin filing out amid many conversations and greetings, I turned to say hello and introduce myself to the elegant couple who had been seated behind my wife and me. I guessed they were in their midseventies.

In response to my name and Sara's, he offered theirs—Joe and Aaronetta Pierce, from San Antonio. More specifically, he said, he was Dr. Joseph A. Pierce Jr., now a retired anesthesiologist. As we talked, I learned that his father had been one of the first African Americans to earn a PhD in mathematics (from the University of Michigan), and his grandfather had been a minister in the African Methodist Episcopal Church and later the Colored (now Christian) Methodist Episcopal Church. His great-grandfather, by the way, he noted, had been George Foster Pierce—the third president of Emory College and, as I well knew, a white man who would later go on to serve as a bishop in the Methodist Episcopal Church, South.

The revelation that a white Methodist bishop had fathered a black son came not so much as a shock (I have no reverence for the slave-owning leaders of early Emory) but more as a confirmation of what many had long suspected. Some historians have surmised that a Jefferson-Hemings kind of relationship might well have formed in Oxford. Suspicions had long focused, however, on Bishop James O. Andrew, the second president, or chair, of the Emory College Board of Trustees.

Although the story of Bishop Andrew and the enslaved members of his household had been told many times, a more complete version of the story had come to light during the Transforming Community Project at Emory, or TCP. In many ways, that ceremony in Old Church that Dr. and Mrs. Pierce attended was the triumphant conclusion of the TCP. The project had been born in 2003 after a moment of racial tension prompted by an incident in a faculty meeting. A highly regarded white faculty member in Emory College—a brilliant researcher, exacting teacher, progressive thinker, and humane spirit—used the most pejorative of racial words while making a metaphorical point. As it happened, the speaker of the word had learned the metaphor from an eminent, chaired professor who was black. But it is one thing for the distinguished black scholar to use the word in pointed irony, and another for a white professor to use it, no matter how ironically. The offending faculty member later apologized for her use of the term and never sought to justify it. Soon, however, the campus had become embroiled in angry letter writing and public forums. Expressions of outrage about insensitivity vied against defense of academic freedom and protected speech.

Two other faculty members recognized the repetition of an old pattern: an offensive action gives rise to community outrage, which in turn leads to institutional apology. The litany has played out on many campuses through the years. Wanting to break through to a new paradigm, to actual learning from the experience, history professor Leslie Harris and journalism professor Catherine Manegold decided to try to help the Emory community chart a different way forward. They suggested turning outrage into education. Certainly, outrage and an answering apology can be appropriate. But, like a downpour after a drought, venting and repentance often provide only short-term relief and fail to address underlying problems of climate change or inadequate reservoirs. When the racial climate on a campus remains unaddressed, or when the community lacks the reservoirs of goodwill and courage to meet the challenges of nasty weather, the institution might try a novel approach to creating a more hospitable atmosphere.

This is what Harris and Manegold proposed. They wanted to devise a way toward knowledge and understanding, if not reconciliation. They urged Emory to go more deeply toward the source of the racial language, stereotypes, and history that undergird how Americans relate to each other across racial lines. Harris, an African American scholar of slavery, and Manegold, a white, award-winning journalist, invited the university to examine its racial history and put it all on record. Only in this way, they reasoned, would subsequent generations of students and others understand that there is nothing new under the sun when it comes to race in America— that outrage and apology and vows to do better have followed in predictable succession at Emory and elsewhere for decades, in part because we have not learned the lessons of our own history.

One of those lessons is that institutions prefer to tell their history in ways that put painful episodes in the best light. Such an episode occurred at Emory in the 1840s and involved Bishop Andrew and an enslaved woman known to her contemporaries in Oxford as Miss Kitty or simply Kitty. We have come to know her by a different name because we know her story more fully.

The narrative handed down by the white community suggested that Kitty viewed her servitude with docile agreeability. Born into slavery, she had been bequeathed to Bishop Andrew by his second wife, with the understanding that Kitty would be offered passage to Liberia at age nineteen. When Kitty reached maturity, Bishop Andrew invited two prominent Emory friends—college president Augustus Baldwin Longstreet and classics professor George W. Lane—to explain to Kitty the options before her: freedom in far-off Liberia or continued service in the home of the bishop. In

the record they put into writing, Longstreet and Lane recounted that Kitty opted to stay in the place she knew rather than risk an ocean voyage to the unknown. All published accounts until the twenty-first century report that the bishop—his hands supposedly tied by Georgia laws prohibiting manumission—benevolently built Kitty a small house (or, in some accounts, gave her land on which her husband would later build a house), where she supposedly lived as free as any white person until her death in 1851, at the age of perhaps twenty-nine.

In *The Accidental Slaveowner*, Mark Auslander has demonstrated through exhaustive research that much of the story about Kitty passed down from the 1840s does not hang together. Questions linger about just how Bishop Andrew came into possession of Kitty and other slaves, and whether the account of Longstreet and Lane's interview of Kitty is fully truthful, and even whether the bishop had a more intimate relationship with Kitty than will ever be known. Perhaps she was the bishop's daughter; perhaps his half-sister, fathered by his own father; perhaps even his mistress.[1]

We who live more than 150 years after the Emancipation Proclamation may have a difficult time making sense of the obviously

Kitty's Cottage, at one time moved to Salem Campground near Conyers, Georgia, and used as a museum to the Lost Cause of the Confederacy, now stands behind Old Church in tribute to the enslaved woman Catherine Andrew Boyd.

confused principles and practices of the Methodist founders of the college. John Wesley, the founder of Methodism, had opposed the slave trade and slavery, and the leaders of Methodism in the American colonies and then the new United States had strongly opposed slavery, writing prohibitions against it into the church's official *Book of Discipline*. Yet Methodism increasingly accommodated the practice of slavery through the first half of the nineteenth century. Methodist attitudes about slavery, especially in the South, were rife with contradictions. Bishop John Emory, for whom both Emory College and Emory and Henry College were named the year after his death, expressed abhorrence of slavery in his diary, yet he came from a prominent slave-owning Maryland family and owned slaves himself—setting them free in his will, which was testated in January 1836, the month after his death in a carriage accident. The founders who built the college 180 years ago set it in the center of a town whose oldest public building is Old Church, a place of worship for a religion whose savior preached a message of freedom. In many ways, though, the church stands symbolically for both the grand intentions of the founders and the flaw inherent in their aims.

For instance, the founders believed they were building a house of worship because their understanding of Providence led them to view that sanctuary as the first step toward a free and hopeful future—for themselves, of course. It is likely that much of the labor to build the church came from enslaved men.

In a way, the building can stand for the society and the institution in which it played such a prominent role. The founders of the college built their church as well as they could, with lines plumb or level, corners true, and wood as hard and well planed as they could find. The windows were clear, not stained glass, and were high and wide to let in the light and beauty of the world while drawing the gaze outward, as if to remind worshipers of the needs of the world. But time and weather and insects and financial hardship or lack of foresight or attention took their toll. By its sesquicentennial anniversary, the Old Church had become downright dangerous, a kind of Dorian Gray edifice whose fine outward appearance belied inner rot.

Twice in the first half of the twentieth century, in fact, the town of Oxford considered razing Old Church, and twice Georgia Methodists devoted considerable funding and energy to save it. By the twenty-first century, the effect of those efforts had waned. The church's foundation sagged, pulling beams out of line, putting stress

where it could not be sustained. Despite an outwardly venerable appearance, the Old Church could not offer haven to those who sought refuge there; it had to be closed. Looking for a place to sing of the Rock of Ages, the townspeople found a house built on subsiding Georgia clay. Looking for shelter from life's storms, they found a place ready to fall around them like matchsticks in a strong wind. Hoping to find peace, they found only the anxious fear that their sanctuary might not last until the year was out.

One might say it was no one's fault, really. Those original builders had built as well as they knew how. As in all human devices and desires, however, the original plan was vulnerable to flaws and weaknesses, both seen and hidden, lying dormant until the moment of stress.

One such moment of stress came just three years after the Old Church was dedicated. Bishop Andrew's ownership of slaves became the flashpoint of the quadrennial conference of the Methodist Episcopal Church, held in New York City in 1844. Northern delegates

Old Church, built in 1841, served as the locus of religious life for both the town of Oxford and Emory College until the construction of Allen Memorial in 1910. Never owned by Emory, the church is now owned and cared for by the Oxford Historical Society, though it continues to serve as the site of occasional programs for Oxford College of Emory University.

to the conference insisted that church policy prohibited clergy ownership of slaves and that Bishop Andrew should either free his slaves or step down. Southern delegates, including some faculty and trustees of Emory College, insisted otherwise. The debate lasted a month. In the end, the southern and northern branches of the church divided. The split presaged the coming Civil War.

To the extent that the Old Church represented a covenant not only between Georgia Methodists and God but also between Georgia Methodists and northern Methodists—and even a covenant among Georgia Methodists themselves, who were somewhat divided on the issue of slavery—the structure may have felt the trembling of some invisible fault line when that union snapped. The split in the church would not be mended for nearly a hundred years.

Meanwhile, the cabin of the young woman, Miss Kitty, whose innocent presence brought the fissures to light, stands just behind the chancel wall of the church. It stands as a reminder of the codicils or reservations attached to every covenant—add-ons or afterthoughts, often unstated, but destined in some way to make the covenant more difficult to live up to than any human being can know.

They did the best they knew how, those early Georgia Methodists. They built the church, the college, the town according to their best lights. With hindsight, we can see how dim those lights were. They could not illuminate the impossible complications of a society founded on the proposition of equality but maintained by the enslavement of an entire race. The knots of logic were so tangled, the consequences so lasting and grave, that they were beyond human capacity to untie. Not without a civil war.

Or, in the case of Old Church, not without recognizing that the building—like the nation—rested on a faulty foundation. It would cost $1 million to repair.

And that is the problem. How can you go back and lay the foundation stone better, once the building is there in front of you? How can you erase a history that continues to plague individuals, communities, and the nation itself—or if not erase it, then rectify it?

Make the question sharper, cutting closer to home. Give every human enterprise the benefit of the doubt—every business corporation, every government, every reform movement, every artistic collaboration, every new religious community—all meant for good, all built into a suitable structure or habitation, a place for haven and security and comfort and happiness, all intended to foster a certain "habit of being" in the world, to use Flannery O'Connor's fine phrase. A place for "service of humanity," in the words of the Emory mission statement. All such enterprises, ultimately, are flawed. All are bound to end up like Old Church, needing either to be extensively renovated, if there's money, or simply knocked down if there's not. For everyone's sake, it would be simply better, safer, easier to torch the old place and start over from scratch.

Here we are, though, in the twenty-first century, wrestling again with the old questions of race in America, having to build out of "the crooked timber of humanity," as Kant called it, a structure as straight as we can make it. What do we do with the racist past of an institution that strives to serve humanity?

Perhaps the best we can do is remember the complications and strive not to re-create them ourselves. And we can offer our regret, on behalf of our institutional ancestors, for the pain and injustice that continue to reverberate down the generations to our own day. This is what the Emory University Board of Trustees did on that day in 2011 when I met Dr. Pierce. They offered a statement of regret. President Wagner read it to the assembled people, who included more than one descendant of enslaved persons in the early Emory community. In addition to Dr. Pierce, the audience included the great-great-great-granddaughters of Miss Kitty—Catherine Andrew Boyd, to use her married name. Cynthia and Darcel Caldwell, her direct descendants, traveled from Philadelphia, Pennsylvania, for the occasion and were presented medals that they received on behalf of their ancestor, who had been named one of the 175 Makers of Emory History being celebrated in that year of observing the university's 175th anniversary.

The trustees' statement read this way:

> Emory acknowledges its entwinement with the institution of slavery throughout the College's early history. Emory regrets both this undeniable wrong and the University's decades of delay in acknowledging slavery's harmful legacy. As Emory University looks forward, it seeks the wisdom always to discern what is right and the courage to abide by its mission of using knowledge to serve humanity.

That statement will not atone for all guilt or assuage all pain. It does not even provide much in the way of details about the skewed foundation of human relations on which Emory College was built. Nevertheless, if we hold that statement before us, we may be able to remember how far we have come and take courage in stepping out toward how far we have yet to go.

CHAPTER 3

Aerial Campus Views

VIEWED FROM THE SKY, Emory through the decades shares with most of America a pattern of ever-increasing encroachment of the built environment into forest, meadow, and marsh. Nowadays, Google Earth makes it easy to chronicle through satellite imagery the advance (and occasional retreat) of human construction from year to year. In earlier decades, the measure was harder to come by, except by airplane flyovers and imprecise comparative perspectives. Nevertheless, the early aerial images of Emory University tell a compelling story.

Hidden from view at this height is a history of the landscape that, even at ground level, few remember. Little trace remains of the Creek Nation who originally inhabited this area: no place names, no historical markers. All that is left of their presence is the traffic pattern around the Druid Hills campus—winding Clairmont Road, North Decatur Road, and Briarcliff Road all follow the paths of ancient trails that white settlers found when they arrived in the 1820s. Nor is there much evidence of the history of slavery in this place. One historical marker on Clifton Road, near Emory's Schwartz Center for Performing Arts, notes that Judge James Paden once had a plantation here; in the 1830s, his plantation house stood near where the clubhouse of the Druid Hills Golf Club now stands, a short drive from the Administration Building at Emory. All this history lies beneath the carefully tended grounds of the Druid Hills campus and requires imagination to unearth.

Imagination, too, produced the first images of Emory from the sky. In the nineteenth century, surveyor Edward Lloyd Thomas drew up a plan for the new town of Oxford in 1837, a year after

Emory College received its charter and a year before the first students showed up for classes. In the twentieth century, architect Henry Hornbostel designed the plan for the Atlanta campus.

Undeterred by the fading fortunes of the Manual Labor School they had founded in 1834 just outside Covington, Methodists in 1836 set their sights on creating a college in a new town nearby. Buying up 1,400 acres north of Covington, they chartered a town they named Oxford, in honor of the university that had educated the founders of Methodism, John and Charles Wesley. In the town

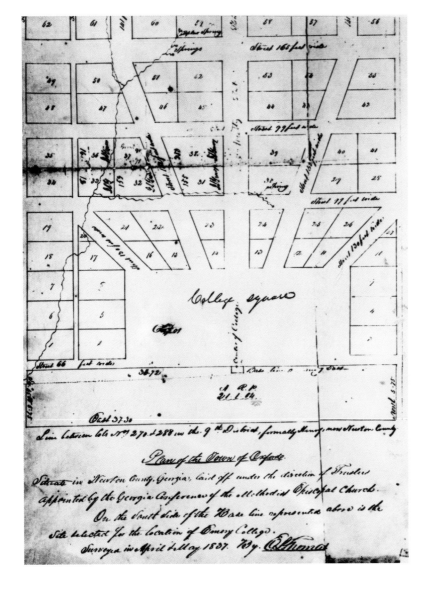

Oxford Town Plan, 1837.

According to Joseph C. Moon Jr., a resident historian of Oxford College and its long-time dean of campus life, a hot-air balloon made possible this aerial photo of the Oxford campus. The date of the photo is probably around the time of the 1919 move of Emory College to Atlanta. The building in the lower left corner is Haygood Hall, named for the eighth president of Emory and constructed in 1913. Note the unpaved campus drives and town streets in the photo. Even eighty years after its founding, the college still nestled in a country village far from the perceived temptations and vices of the big city. An unsigned and undated brief history of Emory at Oxford in the nineteenth century notes "the intangible Oxford spirit" that students derived from the bucolic place and from boarding with town families as if living at home. (Emory College General Records, Emory University Archives series 47, box 1, folder 17, Stuart A. Rose Library.)

plan that Edward Lloyd Thomas laid out, all roads seemingly led to the college. The trustees offered lots on a 999-year lease, with the provision that "no intoxicating liquor shall be sold, nor any game of hazard allowed on the lots, under penalty of forfeiture."[1] (The trustees later conveyed title to the lots by sale, with the same provisos against gambling and alcoholic beverages.) The town itself received its charter in 1839, three years after Emory College and one year after the first classes had begun on the new campus in September 1838.

Erik Oliver, an Emory alumnus, artist, writer, and author of two books about Oxford College and its town, has noted that Thomas's plan has streets radiating out from the college campus and crisscrossing in a way that suggests the image of a cross on a hill, with rays of light emanating outward.[2] Perhaps Thomas, a Methodist minister and certainly attentive to the Methodists who commissioned his work, did have such an image in mind as he developed the town plan, although no documentation of his intention exists.

In 1915, another Emory campus would begin to take shape forty miles west, on the outskirts of Atlanta. Even before Emory University received its new charter from DeKalb County on January 25, 1915, the trustees of the university sought out the right person to design a campus. The beauty and elegance of the design would have to match the founders' aspiration for the university's academic life. The original seventy-five acres, given by Asa Griggs Candler Sr., abutted the suburb of Druid Hills that Candler was developing with his friend and business partner Joel Hurt. Six miles from downtown Atlanta, the acres straddled two hills divided by several streams and covered with pinewoods. To turn this rural landscape on the edge of Atlanta into a university campus, the trustees hired the Beaux Arts architect Henry Hornbostel.

One of a generation of American architects who guided the transition from classicism to modernism, Hornbostel stood preeminently among the Beaux Arts greats. His bridges grace the skyline of New York City, his civic buildings rise majestically in cities on both coasts, and his churches and synagogues are among his twenty-two projects listed on the National Register of Historic Places. (Five of those twenty-two are at Emory: the Old Theology Building, Carlos Hall, Callaway South and North, and Dobbs Hall; two others—the Scott Anatomy Lab and the Fishburne Physiology Lab—were too far removed from the Quadrangle to be included when the Emory Historic District was added to the National Register on November 20, 1975.)[3] Hornbostel had recently completed a design for the Carnegie Institute in Pittsburgh (now Carnegie Mellon University) when the Emory trustees called on his genius.

Having spent time in Italy, Hornbostel found the hills and pines of the Emory terrain reminiscent of the Italian Piedmont. With a nod to that region and to the Piedmont of Georgia, he created an Italian neo-Renaissance design. The red-tile roofs, extended eaves, Roman arches, and marble cladding are characteristic features that continue to distinguish new campus buildings. The unusual pink marble, quarried near Tate, Georgia, was the suggestion of Colonel Sam Tate, a university trustee who owned the quarry.

Using bridges to cross the streams and connect the hills, Hornbostel laid out the academic heart of the campus on a hill that is now the Quadrangle, with a farther hill set off to accommodate living, dining, athletics, worship, and other social activities. While the design proved too expensive to implement fully, the first buildings, opened in 1916, included the Theology Building and Law Building (now Carlos Hall) and the Physics Building (now Callaway Center South). The sole residence hall designed by Hornbostel and still standing is Dobbs Hall (see page 149).

Atlanta campus plan by Henry Hornbostel.

BIRDS EYE VIEW
EMORY UNIVERSITY
ATLANTA GEORGIA

· EMORY · VNIVERꟻITY · ATLANTA · GEORGIA ·

The dramatic elegance of Hornbostel's beaux arts style is apparent in this view of his proposed central tower with flanking colonnades and buildings. Hornbostel intended the tower to house the library and administrative offices, but Emory's trustees decided the tower would cost too much.

The university remained relatively faithful to Hornbostel's template of red-tile roofs and Roman arches for Emory's first half century in Atlanta, even when economy required use of stucco rather than marble in the expansive 1950s and 1960s. Architects strayed wildly from the plan in the 1970s and 1980s, however. Those decades brought the Brutalist style of White Hall and the Atwood Chemistry Center, the modernism of Paul Rudolph's Cannon Chapel, and the large commercial look of Clinic Building B, now blocked from view by the J Wing of Emory University Hospital.

In recent years, university planners have managed to disguise much of the concrete Brutalism of the Atwood Chemistry Center by building Hornbostel-inspired additions around it. White Hall, which some have described as a "workhorse of a building" for Emory College, noting that there's no disputing taste, remains for most a concrete blot on the periphery of the Quadrangle.

This photo, from late 1921, shows why the late biology professor Woolford B. Baker 1920G, for whom Baker Woodlands is named, found the campus a rich resource for environmental study when he arrived in 1919. Just six miles from downtown Atlanta, the campus had a rural aspect, as the woods and fields of DeKalb County stretched north and east of Druid Hills. The two buildings swathed in scaffolding in the upper right corner are Wesley Memorial Hospital, later renamed Emory University Hospital. The hospital and its nurses' training program—later the nursing school at Emory—had been established in downtown Atlanta in 1905 by Georgia Methodists, with significant financial support from Asa Candler Sr. The buildings in this photo, completed in 1922, replaced the old Calico House, the original home of the hospital (see page 176).

Two campus landmarks help date this photo precisely—one by its presence, the other by its absence. Glenn Memorial Church (see also page 136), in the lower center of the photo, constructed in 1931, was the gift of board chair Charles Howard Candler Sr. 1898C 1902M and his wife, Flora Glenn Candler. The building is named for her father, Wilbur Fisk Glenn, who attended Emory College from 1857 to 1859 and served in the Methodist ministry for half a century. Home of the Methodist congregation that had grown up in the Old Theology Building chapel, the acoustically brilliant space doubled as the university's principal performing arts center for eight decades, until the dedication of the Donna and Marvin Schwartz Center for Performing Arts in 2003. Missing from this photo is the water tower installed in 1933, shown on page 200.

The end of World War II and the benefits of the GI Bill sparked an unprecedented growth in the student body and faculty at Emory. To accommodate all the new people, the university built in a frenzy while using trailers and wooden barracks for temporary relief of space needs. The forest began to give way, and with it went some of the sense of leisure about the place. An administration intent on moving Emory into the ranks of research universities understood the need to replace trees and lawns with more buildings for laboratories, study, and instruction. The History Building (1951, now Bowden Hall) in the center of the photo (lower arrow) and the Woodruff Memorial Research Building (1952, upper arrow) to the left of the hospital help date this photo. Missing still is the Administration Building (1955), which would close off the western end of the Quadrangle, still very wooded here. Despite the rapid pace of construction after World War II, alumni from that era returning to campus in the 1980s and 1990s would remark on how much more wooded the campus had been in their day—comments that revealed that the construction had never abated.

Few images reveal as starkly as this one how fields became a residential neighborhood, which in turn gave way to institutional buildings. The intersection in the upper-left corner is North Decatur and Clifton Roads. The large building at the top center is the C. L. Fishburne Building (see page 194), flanked by the old annexes (page 201) where the Schwartz Center for Performing Arts now stands. Harris Hall (page 157) peeks above trees to the right. In the 1970s and 1980s, Gambrell Hall, sorority lodges, and Clinic Building B replaced the houses across from Harris and Fishburne. All of the apartment buildings in the lower half of the photo were on land now occupied by parking decks.

As the Baby Boom hit Emory in the mid-1960s, the campus began to sprawl. Here Cox Hall appears above the hospital buildings, and off to the right edge rise the new buildings of the Center for Disease Control (the CDC, later the Centers for Disease Control and Prevention), which moved to Clifton Road in the 1950s. The presence of the CDC would abet the development of new programs in community health and public health in the medical school, leading in 1990 to the establishment of the Rollins School of Public Health. Missing from this photo is Robert W. Woodruff Library, which in 1969 would take another large bite out of the woods toward the lower left corner of the photo.

CHAPTER 4

The Trees in the Forest

FORGIVE MY PRESUMPTION, but one way to tell the story of Emory's changing landscape is to reminisce about my own experience of that transformation. Yet telling my personal history of Emory—the ways my life has intersected with the university's for more than thirty-five years—might appear to many, as it does to me, too self-focused. Still, every moment of my life at Emory, and every place on campus, points me in some way to the history of the institution itself. Perhaps everyone who has lived or worked at the place could say that. We are all connected by precedent and legacies to the generations who came before, and we are all informed physically by the contours of the land we walk and the shapes of the spaces we fill. My story, then, merely serves to invite you to reflect on your own rich story.

I might begin anywhere: in the Old Theology Building, for instance, where the pungent aroma of centuries-old paper filled the rare-book room behind the desk where I worked for several years in Pitts Theology Library; or at the steps of the Administration Building, where Mikhail Gorbachev walked to the Commencement stage to deliver the keynote address in 1992, the year after I received my PhD degree in the same place; or on the platform of the Depot, where I ate my first Emory lunch in the spring of 1983 with a professor who once caught a passenger train there for a journey to Yale; or at the environmental sculpture whose planks I used to walk with my young children as we descended into the ravine behind the museum after their preschool mornings at the Glenn School.

I begin, though, with the oldest living inhabitants of the place—the trees. How old some of them are, it's hard to say. Those whose age we know, however, have stories and legends worth sharing. Here is one unique arboreal legacy.

In the town of Oxford, Emory College students banded together in 1837 to form the Phi Gamma literary society. In 1851, if the records are accurate (never a sure bet about the college in those days), the Phi Gammas completed their hall on the northwest corner of the college green. (The green would later be termed the Quad, echoing the use of the Druid Hills campus, although the Oxford Quad remained rather round until new construction in the 2010s squared it off.)

At the turn of the new millennium in 2000, nearly a century and a half after the building first opened its doors, Phi Gamma Hall had aged poorly. The oldest academic building owned by Emory, it had resounded with the debates of young men arguing the finer points of women's suffrage, emancipation, Napoleon's greatness, and other topics of the day. The hall had even served briefly as one of the structures of Hood Hospital, which cared for the wounded and dying after the Battle of Atlanta in 1864.

By 2000, architects and engineers reported that only major structural repairs would keep the building usable. To preserve this bit of architectural and campus history, the university spent a year giving it a major makeover. The work led to a fascinating discovery. It turned out that a wooden beam holding up the floor of Phi Gamma had to be replaced, and when workers removed the beam and counted the rings of the tree it once had been, the rings numbered more than two hundred. Assuming that the tree from which this beam was shaped had been felled in 1850 or 1851 for the then-new building, and counting backward for the number of rings, someone calculated that the tree had taken root before 1650—nearly a century before the colony of Georgia received its charter, and nearly two centuries before Emory College enrolled its first students. Harvard College would have been fourteen years old, and Cotton Mather not yet born.

I do not know whether anyone thought to give thanks for the life of that tree when it was cut down in 1850. More likely, the woodsman who felled it viewed it as an infinitesimally small part of the continent's inexhaustible supply of lumber. The earliest images of the Druid Hills campus show the beginnings of a school in a forest. This had been the sense of the founders of Emory College in Oxford as well. The groves of academe were filled with actual trees for many years in both places. Alexander Means, one of the first faculty members of Emory and its fourth president, described the dedication of the first campus building at Oxford this way: "The spot selected for the erection of the first building was on virgin soil, in the midst of a wide-spread and luxuriant forest of native oaks.... The sun shone in splendor from above, and the earth beneath was robed in its garniture of green."[1]

Gradually, the growth of the college and later the university took its toll on the trees, the woods, and the forest canopy. In the 1830s and early 1840s, the town of Oxford was mostly a forest, and as roads and housing lots were carved out of the woods, scores of trees had to be cut. Students sometimes earned money by chopping them down. By 1844, deforestation had reached the point where the town council declared it illegal to cut a tree without permission; scofflaws risked a three-dollar fine.[2] In the earliest days of Emory in Atlanta, the founders of the new university found altogether too many trees. Building a campus required setting up a sawmill near the current Rita Anne Rollins Building of the theology school to take advantage of the board feet growing all around. As late as the 1960s, large stands of pine and oak provided students and others a sense of being far removed from the city only a few miles away.

By the 1980s, though, the prospect of never-ending construction and development—and lessons from the intensive deforestation of much of Atlanta—gave birth to a sense of urgency about preserving natural resources that could never be replaced once they were gone.

Nancy Seideman, for more than two decades the chief media relations manager at Emory and a longtime leader of Friends of the Emory Forest, tells the story of "the greening of Emory" in a chapter of the book *Where Courageous Inquiry Leads*.[3] Briefly, the story is this: a plan to build a road through Lullwater in 1996 galvanized an effort to preserve the woods of the campus with specific policies. The woods and meadows and lake in Lullwater Preserve surround the English Tudor–style house that Walter Candler built in 1925 (see page 75). Originally more than 185 acres, the estate lost a bit of space in the 1960s when Emory conveyed part of it to the federal government for the Veterans Affairs Hospital on Clairmont Road and dedicated another chunk to the Yerkes National Primate Research Center, part of Emory.

When Walter Candler sold Lullwater to Emory in 1958 for $5 million, headlines hailed the estate as breathing room for Emory, a phrase that suggested the possibility of future development there.[4] Perhaps the threat was always present, but in time, some university

citizens recognized the rare gift of this large swath of greenery in the midst of an increasingly congested urban sprawl. William H. Murdy of Emory College and Eloise Carter of Oxford College, both biology professors, prepared an extensive report on the unusual, sometimes unique, qualities of what they termed "the Emory forest"—a remnant of the original Piedmont forest that once stretched across the Piedmont region of the southeastern United States. The Murdy-Carter Report became the touchstone of environmentalists on campus.[5]

At the same time, Emory administrators were recognizing the need for still more room to expand. An apartment complex on forty-two acres across the South Fork of Peachtree Creek from Lullwater beckoned. Nestled between Lullwater and the VA Hospital, these acres ironically had once been part of Candler's estate before he sold them to the apartment developer in the 1940s. Emory bought the apartment complex with the intention of housing graduate students until the aging buildings could no longer serve, at which time, presumably, the university would tear them down and

In the 1930s, Pierce Drive (now called Dickey Drive) appeared to be a road through the forest. Dobbs Hall hides behind the trees to the left of the top of the hill. In a couple of decades, the Geology and Biology Buildings, now Anthropology and Tarbutton, would replace the trees to the right.

build something else in their place. Within a decade, the first step in redeveloping those acres took the form of a parking deck that could hold 1,800 cars. It was grand enough and just different enough in appearance from the usual utilitarian parking deck for students to dub it "Garage Mahal." The deck had ample parking for employees of Children's Healthcare of Atlanta at Egleston Hospital, in addition to Emory employees and students.

The question quickly arose: how could drivers parking in the deck get efficiently to their places of work a mile away? Shuttle buses going the long way around on city streets could take as much as twenty minutes and would make traffic even more congested than it already was. A dedicated road, on the other hand—skirting the edge of Lullwater—would speed the process and take Emory traffic off neighboring streets. Sure, some trees would be lost. Some pathways of animals living in the woods would be paved over. A conundrum arose: for the sake of the environment, would it be all right to disrupt the environment, at least in part?

From this and other proposed developments, the University Senate Committee on the Environment gained determination, strength of voice, and stature in asking difficult questions about the university's stewardship of important natural resources. In time, although the university did build the shuttle road, the board of trustees agreed to implement a policy that guaranteed "no net loss of tree canopy" from construction. For every tree removed from campus, Emory must plant new trees using a formula based on the trunk diameter of the lost tree.

So the forest will endure, and the tree canopy now has its policy and protectors, and that's worth cheering about. Yet what interests me here is not the forest but the trees—those pole-straight loblolly pines that stand like lonely sentinels here or there, or the thick-trunked oaks that guard the Quadrangle, or the white-blossomed ancient magnolias that screen the Baker Woodlands.

Some of these arboreal individuals have gained enough eminence over time to have earned their own name. Some, so to speak, have their own family tree. Take the Yarbrough Oak. In the town of Oxford, just three blocks from the college campus, a white oak (*Quercus alba*) stood for 180 years, having taken root around the time Walt Whitman and the future Queen Victoria were born. According to tradition, the Reverend John Yarbrough— father-in-law of future Emory College president Atticus Greene

Haygood—venerated this tree as the "Prince of the Forest," perhaps harking back several decades to the time when the whole town sheltered under a canopy of green. In 1929, more than a century after the oak burst from its acorn toward the sunlight, the Oxford town commissioners recognized its venerable age by giving the oak a deed for the small plot of ground on which it stood. No one could own this tree, which now owned itself. The celebration of this oak, which in some ways embodied a sense of the history of the college and the town, lasted for another seven decades. A marker identified it as one of the stops on a self-guided tour of the town.

Alas, by 1999, suffering from the stress of increasing urban encroachment, the Yarbrough Oak, as it was called, could no longer thrive. It was cut down, but not before its acorns were harvested and propagated to produce seedlings. Some three hundred of these seedlings have taken root in other sites throughout Georgia. Descendants of the Yarbrough Oak now cast shade all over the state. The Prince of the Forest has propagated a forest's worth of oaklings.

Another oak that bore its own name once stood in front of Emory University Hospital on Clifton Road. It was already there in 1921, when the university built the first hospital structures on Clifton to accommodate the move of its teaching hospital, Wesley Memorial (later renamed Emory University Hospital), from downtown Atlanta to the suburban campus. Certainly the tree was mature in the 1940s, when expansion of the hospital threatened a lovely grove. F. Phinizy Calhoun Sr., chair of the Ophthalmology Department and scion of a great Emory medical family, objected.[6]

Shortly after retiring in 1940, Phinizy Sr. learned about a plan to remove the grove of trees. Alarmed, he argued successfully to retain one magnificent specimen, whose branches shaded the main entrance to the hospital. In 1964, the university affixed a plaque to the tree and named it the Calhoun Oak to honor its guardian. The tree survived for almost another half century, until 2011, when an infestation of ambrosia beetles gave it a death

F. Phinizy Calhoun Sr., 1912.

sentence.[7] Although no Calhoun seedlings exist, Campus Services staff members saved the wood from the tree for local artists to turn into bowls, pens, and other keepsakes.

Consider, too, the many offspring of the East Palatka holly planted by Antoinette Candler. A story passed down through the decades recounts a visit by Bishop Warren Candler to St. Simons Island with his wife—Nettie, as the bishop called her—sometime during his chancellorship of the university. (He was chancellor from 1915 until his retirement from the job in 1920.) Both John and Charles Wesley, the founders of Methodism, had ministered to American Indians and English colonists around Savannah and on the barrier island St. Simons in 1736, shortly after the founding of the colony of Georgia. The Wesley brothers often preached outdoors, and tradition held that one particular large and impressive live oak tree on St. Simons had shaded the young Charles Wesley during a service of prayer and preaching. Some claimed that John later preached there also. The tree came to be known as the Wesley Oak, and a photo of it from 1921 resides on the internet and appears in Lucian Lamar Knight's *Georgia Landmarks, Memorials, and Legends.*

In a pilgrimage to that live oak with her husband, Nettie spotted a small holly bush growing out of a crook of one of the tree's massive, twisting branches—likely from a seed left by a visiting bird in droppings where shallow dirt had accumulated in the bend of the branch. According to lore, Nettie uprooted the little holly and brought it back to Atlanta for transplanting on the Emory campus near the Old Theology Building. Years later, that holly had to be cut down to make way for new steam pipes under the Quad. Groundskeepers took cuttings from it first, then rooted them and planted them around the campus. Here and there (in front of the Psychology and Interdisciplinary Sciences Building, for example, and at the corners of Bowden Hall and Candler Library, and around Glenn Memorial), descendants of that original East Palatka holly bush, the Wesley Holly, still flourish on the campus.

Encounters with the Wesley Holly still produce good stories. A faculty member with whom I shared the story of Nettie and the holly told me his own experience with one of the holly's offspring. Jon Gunnemann had come to the theology school from Yale as a professor of ethics in the fall of 1981 and found himself appointed to the University Senate Campus Development Committee. Sometime in the spring of that first academic year, he received a call from the committee chair, Clyde Partin Sr. 1950C 1951G (Doc, as he was known), the longtime athletics director. Doc told Jon that the committee had received a request to endorse removing a large holly tree on the middle of the Quad; it seemed that the tree, which stood about halfway between the Old Theology Building and Carlos Hall, not only was regarded by some as unsightly but also got in the way of additional seating for Commencement. Doc had polled the committee, and the vote was evenly split. Jon's vote was needed to decide the tree's fate. Would he vote to remove the tree or keep it?

Jon declared that he couldn't decide without at least looking at the tree, which he didn't recall seeing before. So he dutifully strolled from his office onto the Quad, and there it was. Ugly, he thought—it should come down. But as he got closer to it, he saw that the tree bore signs of age: scars from pruning, gnarls that bespoke survival—evidence of a long life on guard over the Quad. Woodsman, spare that tree, he thought.

As Jon stood pondering whether to vote for swinging the axe or sparing the tree, the president of the university approached him. "Jon," said the president, "what are you doing?" Jon explained his mission. "Well, Jon," said the president, "don't worry too much about it. The tree is coming down."

And, thus, the holly fell to "shared governance."[8]

That same western end of the Quadrangle where the gnarly holly stood also nourishes giant pecan trees. They reach a hundred feet into the sky and spread their airy, meandering branches across a diameter of seventy-five feet or more. Legend says that Nettie Candler also planted these trees. Their shade provides relief to the Commencement audience every May, and in the fall men and women and children slowly walk circles beneath their leaves while peering at the ground before stooping to retrieve fallen nuts.

Nettie herself was something of a landscape gardener, by all accounts—the first in a long line of stewards of the campus who have dedicated themselves to keeping it green and beautiful. Under her guidance the ravine behind the old law school building (now Michael C. Carlos Hall) was turned into a garden with an amphitheater spacious enough to serve as the site for Commencement in the 1920s. Called Antoinette Gardens in her honor, the area reverted to wildness after the Commencement ceremony moved elsewhere in 1926.

One faculty member who prized the wild beauty of that ravine and other parts of the campus was Woolford B. Baker. He arrived at Emory in 1919 as a student in the newly formed graduate school.

This was the same year in which Emory College moved from Oxford to Atlanta to join the professional and graduate schools. After earning his master's degree, Baker stayed on as an instructor and later professor of biology (he took two years in the 1920s to earn a PhD at Columbia University). After a long and distinguished career (he was the first recipient of the university's highest annual faculty honor, the Thomas Jefferson Award), he "retired" to serve as part-time director of the university museum, now the Michael C. Carlos Museum. Later in life, Baker recounted the muddy, wooded campus of his student days and the attractions of the swampy places, the wildflowers, the streams and glades that offered a natural laboratory for a young biologist. He planted the magnolias that have grown to specimen size along the western rim of the ravine that now bears his name, Woolford B. Baker Woodlands.

Of the planting of trees, Emory cannot now get enough. Emory plants trees to celebrate new presidents—for James W. Wagner in 2004, a white oak near the Administration Building, the state tree of his native Maryland; and for Claire E. Sterk in 2017, an American elm near the Callaway Center, the closest relative to a Dutch elm to represent her native Netherlands. Emory plants trees to honor departing presidents (a white oak in front of Bowden Hall for William M. Chace in 2003); to recognize distinguished service (a Bloodgood Japanese maple in the garden of the Miller-Ward Alumni House to honor Walter "Sonny" Deriso 1968C 1972L, chair of the $1.7 billion Emory Campaign); and simply to give thanks for trees (a ginkgo, gloriously golden in autumn, between Candler Library and the Callaway Center given by Jean Porter, founding director of the Faculty-Staff Assistance Program, to replace a construction-damaged ginkgo that had been planted decades before by Woolford B. Baker).

For a time, the keepers of tradition even sought to revive a moribund practice from the days of Emory College in Oxford. In that era, the senior class would leave its mark by planting a tree on Arbor Day, which often was held on a different date than the national holiday of April 27. In 1900, for instance, the ceremony took place on February 27; it included prayers, music, "prophecy," a poem, and finally, the planting of a tree, all presided over by the college president and observed by faculty and students.

In the twenty-first century, for a few years at least, the first-year class in the college also planted trees. Departing from Glenn

Memorial after the opening convocation of the year, the class would parade to the Quadrangle for the planting of its own symbol of anticipated flourishing, growth, and branching out, and then would head to nearby tables for ice cream and cold drinks.

Of all the trees on the campus, the one dearest to me is the one near a bench bearing the name of a long-dead university trustee, Granger Hansell 1923C 1924L. Standing in front of the entrance to Carlos Hall, the tree has no plaque at its base to identify it, although many Emory people know its story. The tree is a Nuttall oak. Flourishing since the fall of 2003, it replaced an Overcup oak that had been planted the autumn before. That first oak had fallen victim to boring insects before getting fully established. Something symbolic in that, too, perhaps, because that first tree and its replacement honor the memory of my son, Thomas, who fell victim to disease at the age of sixteen—before really getting established himself. The story of his passing is for another place, but the memory of it brings with it the recollection of an exquisite community who rallied around his family during seven weeks of hospice care in a hellish summer. "The Thomas tree," as many people call it, represents a remarkable chapter of compassion in Emory folks. Two weeks after Thomas's death, faculty and students and friends gathered around that young oak to speak a litany of grace and remembrance. And then a bagpiper—one from the pipe band that leads the Emory Commencement procession each year—skirled the tune of "Amazing Grace."

In some ways, at Emory it is the amazing grace of the trees that keeps the human spirit green. So long as we remember them.

CHAPTER 5

Candler Homes

ASA GRIGGS CANDLER SR., founding patriarch of the Coca-Cola Company, also reared five children whose legacies still redound to the university their father helped to launch. Three sons—Charles Howard, Asa Jr., and Walter—earned degrees from Emory before the chartering of the university in 1915. A fourth, William, was a member of the class of 1911 but did not finish. The only daughter, Lucy Beall Candler, named for her mother, Lucy Elizabeth Howard Candler, attended Agnes Scott College before marrying. (Her first husband died young of a heart attack, and her second husband was murdered in their home, which is now Lullwater Estate condominiums—not related to the Lullwater Preserve of Emory University.) The three oldest sons built mansions that would have formative influences on the development and eminence of the university.

Asa's eldest child, Charles Howard Candler Sr., earned a bachelor's degree from Emory College in 1898 and then studied for a medical degree from the Atlanta Medical College in 1902, thirteen years before the school merged with Emory University to become the Emory School of Medicine. Letters from Asa to Howard, as he was called, fill many folders in the Candler papers in Emory's Stuart A. Rose Manuscript, Archives, and Rare Book Library. In a few, the father takes this oldest son (and Howard's younger brother Asa Jr., called Buddie) to task for not excelling in studies at Emory College as he should, in view of all the benefits he has had as a young man. In time, the first son did very well indeed and became an indispensable lieutenant to his father in managing the family businesses. Like his father, he also became a trustee of the university, and when the patriarch died in 1929, Howard succeeded him as chair of the board, a post he filled until his own death in 1957.

Charles Howard Candler Sr., left, chats with Grady Clay Sr. 1910c at the Centennial Convocation in 1936. Clay, an ophthalmologist in Atlanta when few such specialists existed in the Southeast, created a training program in eye, ear, nose, and throat specialties for Emory medical residents.

To the father's consternation, after he turned over the Coca-Cola Company to his children, they sold it in 1919 for $25 million to a group of investors headed by Ernest Woodruff and W. C. Bradley. Almost immediately, the three oldest brothers began developing baronial estates near the suburb of Druid Hills, where Emory University was beginning to grow. Atlanta businessman Joel Hurt had been developing this area according to a design by Frederick Law Olmsted. Bankruptcy forced Hurt to sell the land to a syndicate headed by his friend Asa Candler in 1908. Candler would go on to complete the work Hurt had begun.

A little over a mile from Emory, on Briarcliff Road, Howard Candler built his own mansion, Callanwolde, in 1920. The name pays homage to Callan Castle, the Candler family's ancestral home in Ireland, conveyed to William Candler by Oliver Cromwell after the suppression of the Irish rebellion of the mid-seventeenth century. (Asa Sr. also owned a mansion in the Atlanta suburb Inman Park that bore the name Callan Castle.) Callanwolde thus combines an allusion to the castle in Ireland with the putative Old English word for "woods," although the etymology is incorrect.

Still, the house was as correct as could be, a beautiful fashioning of English Tudor elements and modern accoutrements set down

One of the early mansions along Ponce de Leon Avenue in Atlanta was Asa Sr.'s own grand house, finished in 1916 and now the home of the congregation of St. John Chrysostom Melkite Catholic Church. Built of yellow brick and trimmed in white, the house earned the appellation of "the lemon cake house" among Candler's children. Photo courtesy of Special Collections and Archives, Georgia State University Library.

in twentieth-century Atlanta. The impact of the house on Emory began when its owner died in 1957. By then, Charles Howard Candler Sr. had served nearly thirty years as chair of Emory's board, had given the funds to build the Administration Building, and had donated with his wife, Flora Glenn Candler, the money to build Glenn Memorial in 1931 in memory of her father (see page 136). Howard Candler's lifetime contributions to Emory totaled some $13 million, or more than $280 million in 2017 dollars. Flora Glenn Candler also was an avid supporter of the arts, and the spectacular Candler Concert Series at Emory memorializes her endowment of musical programs. (For more than sixty years, the series has brought to Emory artists as diverse as Renée Fleming, Wynton Marsalis, Murray Perahia, and the New York Philharmonic.)

After Howard Candler's death, his widow proposed giving Callanwolde to Emory. The university administration studied the feasibility of turning the home into a faculty club, but in the end, the mile-and-a-half distance from campus seemed insuperable—too distant for casual drop-in lunches, too remote for academic programs. Grateful but uncertain what to do with the place, university leaders returned to Flora Glenn Candler and proposed, instead, an endowed distinguished professorship in her late husband's memory. Thus were born

Callanwolde.

The porte
cochere at
Callanwolde.

the Charles Howard Candler Professorships to recognize excellent teaching and world-class scholarship. The first twelve Candler professors were appointed in 1960 and included the renowned philosopher Charles Hartshorne and eminent Civil War historian Bell I. Wiley.[1] The mansion and its twelve remaining acres are now, appropriately, in view of Flora Glenn Candler's passion for art, home to the Callanwolde Fine Arts Center, owned by DeKalb County.

Just up the road from Callanwolde, about a half-mile closer to the Emory campus, spreads the forty-two-acre estate of Asa Candler Jr., whom everyone knew as Buddie. He was a character. His academic indifference was a constant source of grief for his father, but he would prove himself an able salesman for the Coca-Cola Company and later a savvy real estate developer.

Departing from his older brother's sense of architectural refinement, Buddie Candler built Briarcliff, a Georgian Revival mansion with a brick exterior, high columns, and sprawling terraces and gardens. Construction took from 1920 to 1922. Buddie also graced his property with a menagerie of exotic animals: big wild cats (lions and tigers) brought to the estate by truck from the Emory train depot; primates of various species; and at least two elephants bearing names of Coca-Cola advertising—Refreshing and Delicious. By 1935, neighbors' complaints about the noisy and noisome menagerie, as well as possible danger from escaping animals, led Candler to give his animals to the zoo in Atlanta's Grant Park, now Zoo Atlanta. Apparently a congenial host, Buddie devoted himself to throwing entertaining garden parties and opened the larger of his two swimming pools to neighborhood children.[2]

The federal government bought Briarcliff in 1948, reportedly as the proposed site for a VA hospital. Instead of housing health care for veterans, the property became home to a DeKalb County–run treatment center for drug and alcohol addiction and later for the Georgia Mental Health Institute (GMHI), established with the help of psychiatrists in the Emory School of Medicine. By the 1990s, the state had closed the institute and put the property up for sale. Emory acquired it in 1998 for possible development as a biotechnology incubation center in partnership with Georgia Tech. While some efforts in that direction succeeded, for the next two decades the old GMHI buildings largely served as "swing space" for Emory departments in need of a home. In time, the continued deterioration of those buildings led to limiting their use as locations for haunted TV shows like *The Vampire Diaries* and *The Walking Dead*.

OPPOSITE: In this composite of the class of 1899, Asa Candler Jr., "Buddie," appears two photos directly below President James E. Dickey, who is in the center.

SENIOR CLASS
18 99

Moore & Stephenson,   Atlanta, Ga.

Briarcliff in its heyday.

Meanwhile, the mansion fell into grave disrepair. Its listing on the National Registry of Historic Places made it a priority for preservation, but the cost to the university would have been exorbitant. In 2016 Emory and Georgia Tech partnered to build a library service center at the rear of the property. That state-of-the-art facility allows the two institutions to store less-used library materials off campus while making the materials easily retrievable. Despite the high-tech library center, the entire Briarcliff property—from run-down mansion to scary-basement institutional buildings—exerts an eerie appeal to Emory undergraduates seeking a thrill.

Walter Candler, the third-youngest son and fourth child of Asa Griggs Candler Sr. and Lucy Elizabeth Candler, earned his BA degree from Emory College in 1907, then joined his father's bank as

Lawn party at Briarcliff, circa 1950.

Buddie Candler in his TV room.

Briarcliff music room.

an assistant teller, eventually rising to the position of vice president. In the early 1920s, as his brother Howard was building Callanwolde on Williams Mill (now Briarcliff) Road, and his brother Buddie was building the mansion he called Briarcliff, Walter acquired nearly two hundred acres between Clifton Road and Clairmont Road, near what was then the northeast corner of the Emory campus. The area was largely woods and pastures. Lullwater House, begun in 1925 and completed in 1926, was designed by the Atlanta architectural firm of Ivey and Crook, which also designed many of the early buildings on the Emory campus. Built at the then-astounding cost of $200,000, Lullwater has more than 11,000 square feet of floor space, nine working fireplaces, seven full bathrooms, and four half-baths complementing expansive living quarters. Acquired along with 182 acres by Emory for $5 million in 1958, Lullwater has been the official home for Emory presidents since 1963.

Lullwater House.

The South Fork of Peachtree Creek winds down through the center of this photo. To the left is the oval horse track where Walter Candler trained his racehorses and built his paddock and club house. To the right is the lake he created by damming another stream, now known as Ernest Richardson Creek, which flows into the preserve from the lower right corner of the photo. (Richardson was Candler's longtime caretaker of the property, and the stream, named in 2002, was the first space on the Emory campus named for an African American.) Lullwater House perches on the hill above the lake. At the top right, just above the lake, spreads the 1950s-era University Apartments, a privately developed complex built on land previously belonging to Walter Candler. Emory bought these apartments in 1986 and used them for graduate-student housing until tearing them down and developing the Clairmont Campus, which opened in 2002.

The main gateway to Lullwater opens from Clifton Road into Lullwater Preserve, which includes the Emory president's house. Originally more than 182 acres, the estate shrank to about 154 acres after Emory provided land for the Atlanta VA Hospital and dedicated another part of the property to the Yerkes Regional Primate Research Center, now the Yerkes National Primate Research Center of Emory University.

Developed before DeKalb County had installed a county-wide electrical grid, Lullwater initially required its own generating plant, which was housed in this tower. Today a romantic ruin clothed in vines and used by student societies for initiation rituals, the tower originally was graced by clock faces on four sides. In the background, two of Walter Candler's horses graze in the pasture now occupied by the Atlanta VA Hospital.

Before damming Richardson Creek to create what he called Lake Claire (perhaps for nearby Clairmont Road), Walter Candler had a wooden bridge built over the stream. In the distance, an embankment topped by a white fence marks the present-day edge of the lake, now called Candler Lake. The far hills, where Candler grazed cattle, are now entirely wooded. Lullwater House is out of view at the top of the hill that rises to the right of the photo.

Among his favorite pastimes, Walter Candler ranked horses just above reading Shakespeare; he reportedly would host dinner parties at which he assigned guests parts to read from the Bard's plays. Next to the oval horse-training track on the east side of South Peachtree, he constructed this log clubhouse, where he entertained fellow members of the class of 1907 at their twentieth reunion, on June 6, 1927. Candler is unidentified in the photo but may be the man kneeling with the dog.

Front Row
E. A. Rogers
Trammell
Rorie
Hind
John Woodruff
Johnson
Whitehead
Bowon
Rumble
W. Almond *(?)*
Brown

Second Row
Grady Almond
J. L. Adams
Budd
Earl Smith
Burt
T. B. King
Malone
O'Neal

Senior

Third Row
(All others)
Harvard
Candler
Hanson
Council (f)
Harris
John Almond (f)
Barnett (b)

Lassetter
Will Bryan (f)
Stipe (b)
Bray
Lown Jones (b)
Brinkley (f)
Dozier
Duval (f)

Clark
Paul Bryan (f)
Vrisenbaker
Horton
MacGregor

Walter Candler's class of 1907 appears in the earliest extant photo of an Emory graduating class in caps and gowns, in front of Candler Hall at Oxford. (According to Bullock, the class of 1901 had elected to wear academic regalia, but the gowns failed to materialize; Emory graduates first wore regalia in 1902.) Considered for many years a kind of "greatest generation," the class of 1907 included Kemp Malone, later an internationally renowned scholar of medieval English literature named one of the 175 "makers of Emory history" in 2011. Another member of the class was John Gordon Stipe, who had a long and productive administrative career at Emory. The Stipe Society of Creative Scholars, named for him, recognizes six outstanding arts students each year, one each from the fields of creative writing, dance, film, music, theater, and visual arts. Stipe is fourth from the right in the second row; Candler is fifth from the left.

CHAPTER 6

Naming the Streams

THE CHALLENGE—really a supposition or a thought experiment—
was the possibility of walking the perimeter of the Atlanta campus
with your feet always in one stream or another. Frivolously imagi-
native, the notion somehow had allure. A glance at the campus map
suggested the plausibility of the journey. On the other hand, the
pollution in Atlanta-area streams prompted second thoughts. Still,
the prospect of a wacky caper drew us in, conjuring images of Lewis
and Clark trekking with "undaunted courage" through a wilderness
adventure on the edge of an urban university.

The person offering up the notion was John Wegner, long-time
senior lecturer in environmental sciences and at one time Emory's
first "CEO"—chief environmental officer. He was sitting in my faculty-
in-residence apartment at the Clairmont Campus in 2003, sharing
with a dozen students his knowledge of the woods and streams that
make up some 60 percent of the 750 Emory acres between Emory
Village, at the southwest corner of the campus, and the South Fork of
Peachtree Creek, or South Peachtree, which flows along the northern boundary.

The streams themselves are easy to overlook. No fewer than
twelve perennially flowing streams water the Atlanta campus. Most
are small, some now make part of their way through pipes under-
ground, and one or two nearly dry up in the summer. The larger
ones, though, bear Emory history in their names, bestowed on them
in an effort to save them in the early 2000s.

Concerned about the effects of human activity on the quality of
the streams, members of the Ad Hoc Committee on Environmental
Stewardship joined with the Friends of Emory Forest to create the
Stream Naming Committee in 2002. The mission of this band of

earth lovers (of whom I was one) was to solicit the Emory community for suggestions to name four of the twelve streams. The group reasoned that naming the streams would make people more aware of them and thus, perhaps, more likely to treat these vulnerable watercourses with care, finding ways to divert toxic runoff from them, protecting their banks from erosion, and keeping trash out of them.

One half-serious offering alluded to the earliest inhabitants of the area, the Creek Indians. The committee appreciated but rejected the name Creek Creek. Another proposed name memorialized James Paden, an early nineteenth-century DeKalb County judge who owned much of what is now Druid Hills, including parts of the Emory campus. Paden also was a slave owner, and the question arose: was it appropriate to name one of the streams for someone who held other human beings in bondage? The committee consulted faculty members, weighed opinions, and concluded that the name would be fine so long as the history behind it was told and a way could be found to remember those who had been enslaved. In the end, the committee chose another name—that of Ernest Richardson, the African American caretaker of Walter Candler's Lullwater estate during the middle of the twentieth century. Names for other streams paid tribute to architect Henry Hornbostel, longtime intramurals director George Cooper, and Antoinette Candler, the wife of university chancellor Warren A. Candler.

In that conversation with the students in my apartment, Wegner pointed out that two streams—Peavine Creek and South Peachtree—trace the western and northern boundaries of the campus before they meet near the athletic fields named for Walter Candler. Their combined length along the Emory property is some 6,300 meters, or more than 3.5 miles. While they don't encircle the campus, they embrace it like a lobster claw.

So one Saturday in springtime years ago, before many trees had leafed out or mosquitoes sprung forth, a small band of seven or eight began the trek around campus by stream. Not in the water, but on the banks. The point of departure was a now unused bridge that spans South Peachtree, just inside Lullwater Preserve near Clairmont Road.

South Peachtree flows westward under Clairmont Road near the VA Hospital and along the border of the Clairmont Campus before slicing into Emory property near the old electrical generating tower down the hill from Lullwater House. It was in that flat bottom land that Union general John M. Schofield and the Twenty-Third Corps camped in July 1864. Part of the advance of General William T. Sherman's assault on Atlanta, elements of Schofield's army saw action on July 22 in the city of Decatur, two and a half miles away. Confederate cavalry repulsed the Union soldiers but then abandoned the town, giving way to the larger Union force the next day.

According to the late Judson C. Ward 1933C 1936G, historian, longtime Emory administrator, and dean of alumni until his death at the age of ninety-seven, earthworks thrown up by Schofield's army could still be seen around campus as late as the 1960s. What is now the Clairmont Campus became the site of a field hospital after the battle. Up the hill from Clairmont Road (called the Shallowford Trail in 1864), near where the Clifton Childcare Center now welcomes preschoolers, stood a Primitive Baptist meeting house, built around 1830 by one of the early settlers in the area, Naman Hardman. Known as the Primitive Baptist Church in Christ at Hardman's, this building, according to local historian Richard Houston Sams 1957C, was still standing when the Union army marched down the Shallowford Trail toward Decatur. Sams believes the army left the structure in ashes to leave no trace of blood and gore from the field hospital. Three of the four foundation stones on which the meeting house rested are still visible.

Behind the site of Hardman's church, in a grove of trees, lie the graves of some of the county's earliest settlers. Students living in the apartment building just a few yards away from the cemetery frequently move in, dwell, study, make their way to and from class, and move out without ever realizing that their windows look onto the final resting place of human bones.

Sams has written the fullest history of this hallowed ground, and he has good reason for his interest in it—some of his ancestors are buried there.[1] The earliest grave is that of Rody Harriet Hardman, just a year and a half old when she died in 1825. She was the niece of Naman Hardman and the daughter of John Hardman, who was laid to rest near Rody more than half a century later. Not far from the Hardman plot lie Chapmon Powell and his wife, Elizabeth Hardman Powell, parents of Amanda Powell. In 1854, Amanda married Washington Jackson Houston—the builder of Houston Mill and great-grandfather of Richard Houston Sams.

From the Clairmont Campus, South Peachtree skirts past Lullwater Preserve and the home of the Emory University president,

then continues west alongside the Yerkes National Primate Research Center, bends around the hill on which the Houston Mill House perches, and flows under Houston Mill Road into Hahn Woods.

Formally known as the T. Marshall Hahn Commemorative Forest, this Emory landmark honors an Emory trustee and former CEO of Georgia-Pacific. The 4.7-acre preserve was part of a sixty-acre parcel that Emory acquired from the owners of the Houston Mill House in 1960. In the decades immediately after that acquisition, the university covered over a pasture and a swimming pool with construction debris, creating a landfill. In 1993, through a partnership with Georgia-Pacific, which sought to honor its retiring CEO, Emory began reclaiming the site as a teaching area for environmental preservation. Nature trails now lead through a meadow and alongside the creek.

Washington Jackson Houston (pronounced HOUSE-ton) chose this site along the South Peachtree Creek for his mill, for which the nearby road is named. Houston acquired the property in 1842 from his father-in-law, Chapmon Powell, who had settled in the Decatur area in the 1820s and is buried with his wife and other family members in the Hardman Cemetery. Houston dammed the creek to create a sluice for his gristmill, and around 1900 he converted the mill operations from grinding grist to generating

Hardman Cemetery on Emory's Clairmont Campus.

Houston Mill House.

electricity—one of the first generating plants in DeKalb County. In the 1920s, a contractor named Harry Carr, who built the DeKalb County courthouse and Druid Hills High School, acquired the property and resumed gristmilling. He built the Houston Mill House in 1925—the same year that Walter Candler developed his Lullwater estate half a mile upstream. Following Carr's death in 1958—again, coincidentally, the year Emory acquired Lullwater—Emory in 1960 negotiated the purchase of the property from his widow with the provision that she be permitted to live in the house until her death. She died in 1976.

From Hahn Woods, South Peachtree continues west toward the Wesley Woods geriatric center. Those of us making the journey on that spring morning years ago had no easy path here. The woods on the hills beside the stream are lush and come down to the water. We had to pick our way carefully through brush, around boulders, and over fallen logs. At last, though, we reached Wesley Woods. Here, at the northernmost point of its course, the creek bends southwest under Clifton Road and the railroad trestle near Sage Hill.

Vivian Price, in her history of DeKalb County, reports that the area near Sage Hill, where Briarcliff Road and Clifton Road intersect, once was the site of a small village called Wallace.[2] Named for John Wallace, who owned and operated a nearby sawmill until 1900, the village included a handful of stores, a blacksmith shop, a post office, and a railroad flag stop known as Wallace Station. By the time Emory College moved to the Atlanta campus, the village had disappeared, but as late as 1936 the area still retained the name of Wallace Station. It was there that a group of Atlantans intended to erect a memorial to the celebrated Atlanta poet and Emory alumnus Ernest Hartsock 1925C, the first Georgian to receive the annual award of excellence from the Poetry Society of America. Hartsock, a close friend of historian C. Vann Woodward 1930C and founder of Bozart Press, died of pernicious anemia at the age of twenty-seven.

Looping around Candler Field, South Peachtree meets Peavine Creek, which empties into the larger stream to continue toward Peachtree Creek and, eventually, the Chattahoochee River. Peavine Creek meanders to this spot from nearly four miles to the south, after rising from a source near the post office in Decatur. The last mile or so of Peavine Creek forms the western boundary of the Druid Hills campus. The creek flows under North Decatur Road in Emory Village, northward behind the Peavine parking deck, past the western edge of Candler Field, and into South Peachtree. On our trek that spring, our band of adventurers made our way upstream along the eastern bank of Peavine Creek, headed south toward Emory Village.

Peavine itself has several feeder streams from the campus, including Cooper Creek near the Chappell Park baseball diamond, Hornbostel Creek south of the Peavine parking lot, and Antoinette Candler "Nettie's" Creek, which empties into Peavine at Emory Village. Nettie's Creek in fact created the final leg of the watery tour of campus. Following Nettie's Creek upstream, we walked from Emory Village into the grove of trees beside the Oxford Road Building, through a culvert under Dowman Drive, and into Baker Woodlands.

This small wooded preserve conveys a sense of the forest that used to cover the Piedmont region of Georgia. It also is home to the environmental sculpture *Source Route* by artist George Trakas, who received an honorary degree from Emory in 2011 (see pages 171–73). Following Nettie's Creek upstream, walkers can slip under the Mizell Bridge toward the large culvert through which the stream flows under Woodruff Library.

The annual pushball competition usually ended with the student referees being detrousered and tossed into a nearby stream. The event, begun in 1923, pitted freshmen against sophomores, with bragging rights at stake. The administration banned the game after the 1955 clash because of a legacy of physical injuries to participants—and the ignominy of referees made pantsless after matches. I have never been able to determine whether it was Peavine Creek or Hornbostel Creek into which referees of pushball games were tossed after having their pants removed by the winning team.

On the other side of the culvert, in a small grotto, lies the end of the water trail. The source of Nettie's Creek, on the east side of Clifton Road, has long been buried and piped. From somewhere near the law school, conduits direct the stream under streets and buildings to daylight in the grotto next to the library. There, in 2003, reaching into the discharge pipe as far as we could, our expedition left a stack of three quarters—all the change we had among us!— as evidence of our passing. And then we sang the first lines of the alma mater, for we truly were "in the heart of dear old Emory."[3]

Baker
Woodlands.

CHAPTER 7

The Quadrangle

THE STORY OF Emory's refounding in Atlanta has been told at length many times, but here it is in a paragraph. In 1914, angered by a failed lawsuit against Vanderbilt University, which the Methodist Episcopal Church, South, had founded as Central University in 1870, leaders of the denomination severed its ties with Vanderbilt and decided to create a new university in the Southeast. At issue was the question who had the authority to approve appointment of trustees and various policy decisions—the bishops of the church or the Vanderbilt board alone? The Tennessee Supreme Court sided with Vanderbilt. High on the church's list of priorities was a theology school to continue the education of ministers. With the gift of $1 million and seventy-five acres from Coca-Cola magnate Asa Candler, the church decided to build a university in Atlanta. Perhaps not coincidentally, the dollar amount matched the gift from Cornelius Vanderbilt in 1873 that led to the renaming of that university, and the land gift matched the original size of the Vanderbilt campus. Interestingly, the Vanderbilt University website in 2018 noted that Vanderbilt severed its ties with the church, rather than the other way around.[1] History is often a matter of perspective.

In September 1914, the Candler School of Theology—named for Asa and his brother, former Emory president and now Methodist bishop Warren Candler—opened its doors in downtown Atlanta, becoming the first division of the new university to begin operation. World War I had just begun. Emory University itself would not receive its new charter until January 25, 1915. Over the next year, trustees of the new university undertook to carve an educational institution out of woods and fields.

One of the first two academic buildings on the new Druid Hills campus was the Theology Building, which included the chancellor's office, classrooms, faculty offices, and the theology library. In 1976 the university renovated this building for use entirely by the Pitts Theology Library, which had acquired a 220,000-volume collection from the Hartford Theological Seminary to become one of the largest theology libraries in North America. Architect Paul Rudolph designed steel mezzanines and shelves to convert the chapel and another room into reading rooms, and then imposed a color scheme of pink hues to complement the pink and gray marble on the building. When Pitts Library moved into a new home in 2014—coincidentally the centennial of the theology school—the university designated the Old Theology Building for restoration.

Durham Chapel served the theology school—and the university—as a teaching and worship space until its transformation into a library reference room in 1976. This photo shows the theology school at worship in 1954.

For nearly forty years—1976–2014—the deconsecrated and converted Durham Chapel served as the reference room for the Pitts Theology Library, until the library's move to a new building. Besides theology students, college undergraduates found the space a welcoming and quiet place to study—and to nap on the comfortable love seats.

The tall windows of the Old Theology Building could be opened to allow cooling cross-ventilation before the building was air-conditioned. The wooded west end of the Quadrangle is visible through the windows in this photo from the 1930s—woods that would give way to the Administration Building. In 1976, to accommodate the growing periodicals collection, this reading room gained steel mezzanines and shelving, which were removed in 2017 during restoration of the building.

A year after the university received its charter, the Emory trustees observed, in 1916, that the typical law school was merely "over-supplying in numbers the demand for lawyers" in an "over-crowded" profession and failing to meet the demand for "properly trained lawyers." Intent on offering a standard of legal education that would elevate the profession in the Southeast, the trustees created a school that would model its curriculum on that of the elite law schools of the Northeast, notably those at Harvard, Yale, and Columbia (the three schools from which Emory would recruit most of its first law faculty). The trustees named it the Lamar School of Law, after the 1845 Emory College graduate Lucius Quintus Cincinnatus Lamar, who became a U.S. senator and Supreme Court justice. Now known simply as Emory Law, the school spent its first six decades in this building before moving in 1972 to new quarters in Gambrell Hall (see page 134). The original law building, renamed Michael C. Carlos Hall since its 1985 renovation, for a time housed departments of anthropology and sociology as well as art history. Today its east wing is part of the Michael C. Carlos Museum, and art history occupies the west wing.

OPPOSITE: The interior staircase of the Law Building as it appeared until the 1985 renovation by Michael Graves.

John C. Kilgo served as president of Trinity College (now Duke University) before being elected as a Methodist bishop. His connection to Emory came from his service on the educational commission that chose Atlanta as the location for the church's new university, and he served as a trustee of Emory until his death in 1922. Kilgo Circle, named for him, formerly encircled the Quadrangle as an oval. Construction of Woodruff Library in 1969 at the southeastern curve of the oval and of White Hall and Cannon Chapel in the 1970s at the northwestern curve obliterated any sense of the roadway that had once carried traffic and included spaces for parked cars.

Coming around the bend from behind the Old Theology Building, this stretch of Kilgo Circle would be closed off in 1955, when Emory built the Administration Building, at approximately the spot where the photographer stood to take this photo.

This stretch of unpaved road behind the current Carlos Hall still bears the name South Kilgo Circle. The only other part of Kilgo Circle still extant is a walkway, paved in bricks since 1998, that passes in front of the Modern Languages Building and under the overhang of Cannon Chapel next to Rudolph Courtyard. The circle has become two short straight lines, one of them for pedestrians only.

LAW CLASS EMORY UNIV ATLANTA, GA MARCH, 1933

Among the host of distinguished graduates of the law school during the 1930s
was Henry Bowden 1931C 1934L, seated second from right and wearing a sweater.
Bowden went on to become a prominent Atlanta attorney and chair of the Emory
board of trustees from 1957 to 1979. He and his fellow law alumnus Ben F. Johnson
Jr. 1936C 1940L were the guiding spirits in the effort to integrate Emory in 1962,
when the university successfully sued the state of Georgia to overturn racially
discriminatory statutes that limited the right of private institutions to integrate
their student bodies.

Constructed in 1955, this building was the first on campus intended solely for administrative purposes. (The Old Theology Building housed the chancellor's and college dean's offices until 1919, when the newly constructed Physics Building offered more space, and in 1926 Candler Library became the still newer home for these administrators.) The Administration Building lost its roof when an attic fire broke out in September 1956, and four days later the building suffered further insult as Hurricane Flossie drenched the exposed attic. In a letter four years later, business manager Charles O. Emmerich noted that after four years of use, "we find that it would be better suited to our needs if it had been 10 percent bigger." Correspondence of 1962 outlined plans to store newspapers and books in the attic; forty years later, the county fire marshal ordered the attic cleared, and the materials from the attic filled a semitrailer full of paper to be recycled. An October 1968 memo remarked, "All evidence of smoking in the attic has been removed"—a good thing, considering the many books, boxes, and piles of trash vulnerable to another spark. Air-conditioning finally arrived in 1969. In the temperature-controlled work environments of the twenty-first century, it is sometimes difficult to imagine what it was like to spend an eight-hour day in such offices before air-conditioning.

At one time—about 1960 in this photo—the break room on the first floor of the Administration Building had a staff person to serve coffee and snacks. As the university built new office and classroom space in the 1960s and 1970s, planners rarely included such meeting places in their designs. That practice would change after 2000, when a report by the blue ribbon Committee on Traditions and Community Ties at Emory (CONTACT Emory) recommended that every new building contain such areas for informal gatherings and conversation. Subsequent planners have taken pains to include coffee shops and casual meeting spaces in buildings.

The groundbreaking for Cannon Chapel, on August 30, 1979, was the occasion for the first visit to Emory by a sitting U.S. president—Jimmy Carter. It was also, according to President Carter's later recollection, the hottest day of his life. Like others on the platform for the ceremony, he was garbed in the heavy fabrics of traditional academic regalia as he prepared to receive an honorary doctor of laws degree. Perspiration poured from his forehead as he joined President James Laney, Bishop William Ragsdale Cannon (former dean of the theology school and namesake of the chapel), and trustees in turning a shovel of dirt. The ceremony took place at one o'clock in the afternoon on a stage with no awning to protect the dignitaries from the blazing summer sun. A thousand chairs faced the platform. The groundbreaking, according to a memo from Vice President Orie Myers, was at the southeast corner of Pitts Library (now the Old Theology Building); other photos seem to show Bishops Hall in the background, suggesting that the groundbreaking was about where Rudolph Courtyard would take shape behind the Old Theology Building.

Cannon Chapel.

Across the ravine in this photo, the Physics Building rises behind the Chemistry Building in 1951, both buildings now renovated, joined, and renamed the Callaway Memorial Center. The bulldozer in the ravine is preparing the foundation for the Basic Science Building, which would consolidate preclinical instruction for nursing and dentistry students when it was completed. In the following decade, the building became home to the Psychology Department and served as the Psychology Building until completion of the Psychology and Interdisciplinary Sciences Building in 2009. The old Psychology Building is now the Modern Languages Building.

Opened in 1917 to prepare for the move of Emory College to Atlanta two years later, the Chemistry Building began life as a place to instruct medical students in basic sciences. It also began as half of itself—only the bottom two of the planned four stories. The university did not have money to complete it until 1927. After the construction of the Atwood Chemistry Center in 1974, Emory renovated this old building and renamed it the Humanities Building to house the English Department and other humanities programs. Further restoration in 1993 connected it to the former Physics Building, which had been constructed on the Quad in 1919 to house not only the Physics Department but also the bookstore, administrative offices, and the principal classrooms and offices of the college. The new complex, called the Loula Walker and Ely Reeves Callaway Sr. Memorial Center, bears the names of the parents of Ely Callaway Jr. 1940c—founder of Callaway Vineyard and Callaway Golf and one of the "makers of history" honored by Emory during the university's 175th anniversary observance in 2011.

Part of a massive building program in the early 1950s, the History Building filled in the only remaining empty corner of the Quadrangle. Finished in 1951, it was renovated in 1985 and renamed in 1991 to honor Henry Bowden 1933C 1934L, longtime chair of the board of trustees and one of the two principal architects of the university lawsuit against the state of Georgia in the fight for desegregation in 1962. The design of Bowden Hall replicates and pays homage to the features of the earlier Hornbostel buildings on the Quad.

Emory College created a museum for instruction as early as 1876, with collections of gems, shellfish, bird carcasses, insects, and other natural scientific materials. Reportedly the museum at one time also included the first Maytag washing machine in the state of Georgia. The establishment of the university in Atlanta provided the impetus to add to this natural history museum by bringing together other valuable collections, including an archive of rare books and manuscripts from early Methodists. In 1920, Professor William A. Shelton of the theology school traveled to Egypt, Palestine, and Mesopotamia (now Iraq) with a team from the Oriental Institute at the University of Chicago. The crates of materials he bought during the journey and sent home—mummies, sarcophagi, urns, utensils, pottery, and jewelry—were the seeds of what would later become the Michael C. Carlos Museum. In this photo from 1962, an Atlanta school student takes notes about a mummy. The museum was housed in the basement of Bishops Hall from 1957 to 1972, when it moved to what is now Carlos Hall until the opening of the new museum building in 1993. The film director John Huston used the museum for a scene in the 1979 film *Wise Blood*, when a character named Enoch Emery steals a shrunken, three-foot mummy—an artifact never actually owned by the Emory museum.

CHAPTER 8

Commencement

TO UNDERSTAND HOW Commencement at Emory has changed in just the last 30 years, let alone the last 180, imagine the Quadrangle as it looked on May 11, 1987. Paul Volcker, the Federal Reserve Board chairman, received an honorary degree that morning before delivering what must have felt to the graduates and their families like what it was—a long policy talk with a sprinkling of advice but no PowerPoint slides to illustrate or enliven it. Other dignitaries receiving honorary degrees that day included a diplomat, a civil rights activist, a literary scholar, a biochemist, a global health administrator, and an ethicist. Their presence signaled the priorities of the moment for the university, as it expanded internationally, built stronger connections to the city of Atlanta, renewed its commitments to health sciences and public health, and launched a new emphasis on ethics.

A stage jutted out over the steps of the Administration Building into the Quadrangle, and a blue-and-gold awning suspended temporarily from the building shaded the platform party from the sun. This same stage, or one very like it, had graced the same spot since 1959. Facing it, ranks of white wooden chairs ranged back some sixty yards to the sidewalk between Carlos Hall and the Old Theology Building, filling perhaps a quarter to a third of the Quadrangle. Movable bleachers, pulled into place by a tractor a few days earlier, rose behind the last row of chairs to give audience members in the back a line of sight over the heads of those in front. In all, the graduates and their families and friends may have filled four thousand seats.

A few years later, in 1991, Jane Fonda sat in front of my family as I received my PhD degree. She was there not to see me, of course, but to watch her husband, Ted Turner, receive an honorary degree along with Andrew Young, Rosalynn Carter, and that

104

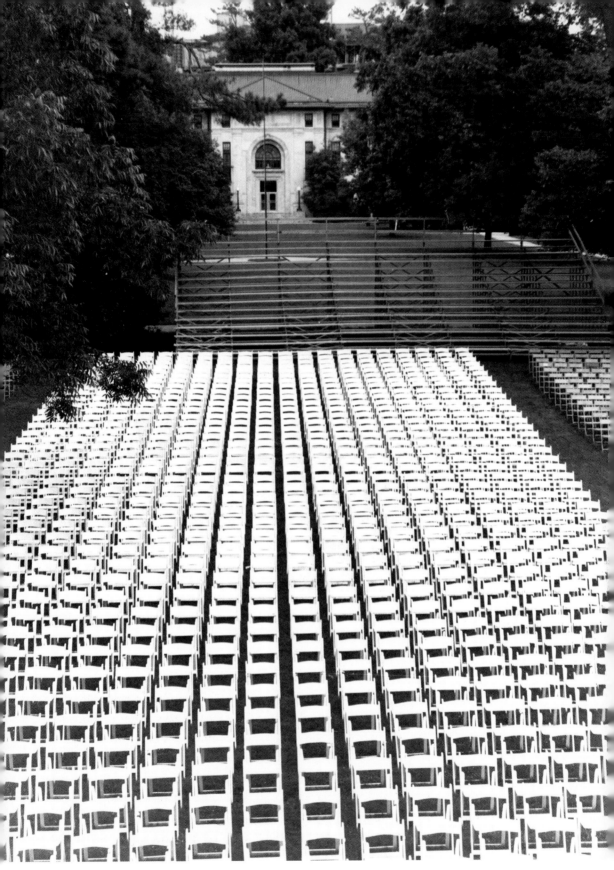

Seating for Commencement during the 1980s required only enough chairs to fill the western quarter of the Quadrangle.

year's Commencement speaker, Eduard Shevardnadze, the last foreign minister of the Soviet Union and later president of the newly independent Republic of Georgia. Shevardnadze's granddaughter, Tamuna Mosashvili 1994C, had entered Emory College as an undergraduate, and the university had already begun a partnership with Georgian medical and educational institutions that would grow in impact over the next decades. A visit from Shevardnadze was thus doubly fitting. That year the rows of chairs stretched back to the flagpole in the middle of the Quad, as 2,320 graduates received degrees. The next year, Commencement would become almost unrecognizable.

By 1991, I had been working in the University Secretary's Office for nearly three years, and in September, President James Laney appointed me as university secretary. The secretary's office ran Commencement, from coordinating the baccalaureate service to arranging special hotel rates for out-of-town families, from writing the honorary degree citations to managing the travel of dignitaries, from hiring the bagpipe band and brass quintet to making sure students lined up in the right place on Commencement morning. Of course, many hands worked to ensure success. I chaired a committee of some thirty persons, who included facilities managers, the chief of Emory police, school and university marshals, the head of the corps of ushers, various assistant deans, and administrators and staff members from a dozen departments. A good and hardworking group that got along well, we were not prepared for what was about to happen in the spring of 1992.

With the dissolution of the Soviet Union during the presidency of Mikhail Gorbachev, the appearance of Shevardnadze had suggested to President Laney a still more interesting opportunity. Just a few years earlier, in 1988, Nobel Prize–winner Desmond Tutu had delivered the Commencement address. What about bringing another Nobel Prize winner, Gorbachev, to Emory?

Out of power in late 1991, Gorbachev had decided to go on a speaking tour of the United States. Among the stops on the tour would be Westminster College, the little school in Fulton, Missouri, where Winston Churchill had delivered his famous "Iron Curtain" speech in 1946. With the Iron Curtain torn and fallen, Gorbachev's speech would bookend an era. When his speaker agency contacted the President's Office at Emory to announce this limited tour, with only half a dozen stops, Laney leapt at the opportunity. The pitch to win one of the coveted stops in the tour was easy: Emory is closely affiliated with the Carter Center, an enterprise launched by another former president (and later Nobel Laureate), and no doubt Mr. Gorbachev would find a conversation with University Distinguished Professor Jimmy Carter instructive as the former Soviet president thought about his future.

When Gorbachev accepted the invitation to deliver the Commencement address and receive an honorary degree in May 1992, the announcement precipitated a mania of interest. Suddenly the University Secretary's Office was receiving phone calls from people in neighboring states asking how to attend a ceremony in which they would have had no other interest. A church in south Georgia wanted to bring a bus full of congregants. Book clubs and social groups wanted details about parking and seating. Media interest was unrelentingly intense. Soon it became clear that we would need more chairs on the Quad. And a fence. And tickets. How else could we ensure that graduates' guests—not to mention the graduates themselves—would have a place to sit?

By May 11, fifteen thousand chairs stretched from the stage at the Administration Building all the way back to Candler Library, nearly

Mikhail Gorbachev greets Emory student Tamuna Mosashvili 1994C, granddaughter of Eduard Shevardnadze, president of the Republic of Georgia, before the 1992 Commencement.

two hundred yards away—nearly four times more chairs than ever before. An eight-foot-high green fence encircled the Quadrangle to help manage the crowd and preserve seats for members of the Emory community. College graduates were limited to six tickets for guests, while other graduates were limited to four. Their consternation and protest hardly abated with the knowledge that they could have any number of guests at their diploma ceremonies—after the main event with its high-celebrity speaker.

It was an altogether magnificent day. Senator Sam Nunn 1961C 1962L introduced President Jimmy Carter, who in turn introduced Gorbachev. The audience heard the Commencement address twice, once in Russian and once in English, as Gorbachev would speak a paragraph then wait for his translator to deliver it. On it went for who remembers how long. No doubt the audience grew restive. Although television monitors halfway back helped a few people see what was happening on the faraway stage, the downward slope of the western third of the Quad meant that those in the rear to the east could barely make out the top of Gorbachev's head—if they could see anything on the stage at all.

Early Commencement exercises were held in Old Church at Oxford, shown here decorated for the 1907 Commencement.

Since the move of Emory College to Atlanta in 1919, the Oxford campus has continued to hold its own graduation exercises before the Commencement on the Druid Hills campus. This photo shows the graduates of Emory-at-Oxford on June 3, 1950, standing in front of Old Church. The lone young woman among the graduates was Dorothy MeGahee, one of only three female students at Oxford at the time, all of them boarding in the town. Women came to Oxford as residential students in 1954, the year after the Emory board of trustees opened the door for female undergraduates to live on campus.

Commencement at Emory has always aimed to be grand. True, the first Emory Commencement, in 1840, had not a single graduating student and consisted wholly of speeches, prayers, and commendations by various dignitaries and students. Not until the following year would three students—Henry Bass, Armistead R. Holcombe, and Adam C. Potter—receive diplomas as part of the ceremonies.

Graduation exercises in those early years went on for days, and the days were long. Typically, Commencement week began with a Sunday morning sermon during worship, more sermonizing in the afternoon, then an evening filled with first-year students reciting famous speeches and poems (perhaps a bit of Ciceronian rhetoric or an ode by Horace—both in Latin, of course). The following day, sophomores offered more of the same, while Tuesday

Remains of the Chaple. Burned August 1916

In 1923, this wooden structure, built as an assembly hall and chapel, housed the first Commencement on the Druid Hills campus.

allowed the juniors to hold forth, each class offering its best declamations to demonstrate their learning from the year just concluded. At last, on Wednesday, attention turned to the seniors, who began at eight thirty in the morning presenting original speeches, often as long as half an hour each, followed by a lengthy keynote address from an honored speaker and an afternoon gathering of the Few and Phi Gamma literary societies for still further orations. All of this took place at Oxford in the heat of mid-July.

The move of the college to Atlanta in 1919 to join the newly formed university prompted years of wandering for the Commencement ceremony. The first school of the university established in Atlanta was the Candler School of Theology, which opened its doors in September 1914 in the Wesley Memorial Church Building downtown, at the corner of Auburn Avenue and Ivy Avenue (now Auburn Avenue and Peachtree Center Avenue). In that building—razed in 1964—three men received theology degrees from the university in June 1915. One of those men was Keener Rudolph, whose son, Paul Rudolph, would later become dean of architecture at Yale and would receive the commission to design Cannon Chapel. The courtyard outside that chapel bears the Rudolph name, honoring Paul Rudolph's gift of the bricks to pave it.

Wesley Memorial continued to host Emory Commencement until 1923, when the addition of more schools in Druid Hills gave greater imperative to a campus graduation ceremony. By that time, Emory College had moved from Oxford, and graduates received degrees in Atlanta for the first time. That year, the Commencement audience gathered in a wooden assembly hall on the spot where the Alumni Memorial University Center (AMUC) now stands.

The next year, everything moved outdoors for the first time. Antoinette Candler had overseen the development of a garden in the ravine behind the Law School (now Carlos Hall), and the university had created an amphitheater out of the hillside there. In 1924 and 1925, students wound their way down a staircase from Kilgo Circle into Antoinette Gardens for the Commencement ceremony. (The stairway no longer exists—or if it does, it's buried under accumulated dirt, leaves, and forest debris left by the woodlands' decades-long reversion to a natural state.)

In 1926, inexplicably, organizers moved the ceremony from the shade of the garden to a tent on the lawn in front of the C. L. Fishburne Building. An earlier Emory historian, Thomas H. English, described the scene as "a blistering hot and humid noonday [and] an occasion to be recalled with horror."[1]

Graduates of the Wesley Memorial Hospital nursing program descend the now-vanished stairs behind the old law building (Carlos Hall) for Commencement in Antoinette Gardens in 1925. The gardens have reverted to natural wildness and are now named Woolford B. Baker Woodlands.

Chief Marshall
J. Sam Guy, professor
of chemistry, leads
the Commencement
procession to Glenn
Memorial in the 1930s.
Candler Library rises
in the back.

In 1927, after the old wooden assembly hall burned down, the university replaced it with a granite dining hall and auditorium, now the western half of the AMUC. There, Commencement audiences gathered until Glenn Memorial opened in 1931.

The gracious, beautiful church became home for the ceremony for a decade until, in 1941, the occasion once again went alfresco. The completion of the Church School Building behind Glenn Memorial in 1940 created space for another lovely amphitheater that would harbor Commencement audiences until the 1950s. Misguided forays took the ceremony once to the athletic field and once more to Glenn Memorial, but at last, in 1959, the Quadrangle welcomed the graduates for a six thirty evening ceremony.

That evening event was not unusual for the period. Most Emory Commencements in the 1920s and 1930s had taken place in the morning, but beginning in 1941, evening beckoned. Perhaps the shade cast by Glenn Memorial on the Church School amphitheater made the space cooler than under the blazing morning sun. In 1964, however, Commencement again returned to morning, and there it has stayed, though with some variation in the starting time. While the day of the week fluctuated through the decades—often falling on a Friday or Saturday, sometimes on a Sunday—Commencement has been held on Monday since 1960. Now anchoring the calendar for the academic year, Commencement is always the second Monday in May, usually (but not always) the day after Mother's Day.

Commencement provided the platform for the first televised event in the history of Emory University. The featured speaker was an alumnus who happened to be serving as vice president of the United States. Alben W. Barkley had already graduated from Marvin College, in his home state of Kentucky, when he enrolled to study law at Emory as a member of the class of 1900. Without graduating, he went on to pass the bar and practice law before beginning a long political career as a congressman and later U.S. senator. In 1949, just five months after his inauguration as vice president in the administration of President Harry Truman, Barkley traveled to Emory to deliver the Commencement address and receive an honorary

Alben W. Barkley spoke to the Commencement audience in the Church School Amphitheater in 1949.

The Commencement audience in 1942 easily fit
into the amphitheater between Glenn Memorial and
the Church School Building. Graduating nurses in
the front rows wore white regalia.

degree. From the amphitheater at the Church School Building, WSB broadcast the vice president's speech, while 787 graduates basked in their gowns in the warmth of a June evening.

The world apparently little noted nor long remembered what Barkley said there. But he did inspire the university the following year to request his permission to name its debate program after him. Thus was born the Barkley Forum, perhaps the finest collegiate debate program in the country, whose participants have won more than their fair share of national championships. (In the 1980s, leaders of the Barkley Forum partnered with Atlanta Public Schools to create the Atlanta Urban Debate League as a way of strengthening the schools and offering rhetoric to replace violence in settling disputes.)

They say it never rains on Commencement at Emory. This is possibly true if you think of droplets falling from the sky as nothing more than heavier-than-usual humidity. In fact, the occasion has had some dicey moments.

In 1996, Spelman College president Johnnetta Cole had just begun her Commencement address on the Emory Quadrangle when moisture began precipitating from the sky. No one called it rain, but colorful umbrellas began popping open among the graduates and out across the rest of the audience. The sprinkling lasted just a minute, and then the sun came out. But Emory president William M. Chace had begun looking for that part of the script that called for a quick conferral of degrees en masse and the cue for exit music.

Before the 167th Commencement, in 2012, a steady drizzle bathed families and friends arriving before dawn to find the best seats among the fourteen thousand chairs. Graduating students and the faculty began the procession with umbrellas aloft, yet almost on command the soaking rain stopped at the moment the platform party stepped onto the Quad.

More than meteorology distinguishes Commencement at Emory, however. One commentator in the nineteenth century, quoting Alexander Pope, described the annual occasion as "the feast of reason and the flow of soul." Festive in spirit and elevated in rhetoric, Commencement week in the nineteenth century was much like a Chautauqua meeting. Audiences came for the speeches and music as much as to celebrate the graduates, and the impact of the annual event on the social and intellectual life of Georgia was profound.

These days the feast and the flow are enriched in many ways by traditions begun not much more than a decade ago, from Class Day to the Senior Crossover, when graduates walk the pedestrian bridge from the Emory Conference Center Hotel to the Miller-Ward Alumni House, marking their transition from students to alumni. On Commencement morning, the skirl of bagpipes and the martial tattoo of drums echo off the Quadrangle buildings as a bagpipe band leads in the procession. They play "The Emory and Old St. Andrews March," composed by Henry Frantz 1974C 1977L. The tune, used every year at Commencement and convocations, commemorates the university's relationship with the University of St. Andrews through the Bobby Jones Scholarship program, which memorializes golfing great Robert T. Jones 1929L. The tune calls to mind the heritage of that great Scottish university, whose own history reaches back more than six hundred years.

Ever since universities first took root as the primary cultivators of new knowledge and ancient wisdom, they have found it necessary to celebrate the achievements of their people by way of the pomp, ceremony, and theater of commencement. Emory relishes the show no less.

The 1936 centennial celebration at Emory included a procession led by these gonfalons, representing the Phi Gamma and Few literary societies. Modern Commencement processions feature the entry of students from the university's nine schools led by their respective gonfalons.

Bagpipers have led the procession at Commencement,
convocations, and special ceremonies since the 1970s. Here
the Atlanta Pipe Band, with Henry Frantz 1974C 1977L in the
foreground, precedes the procession to Glenn Memorial for the
1986 sesquicentennial convocation.

Much of the pageantry of modern Commencement exercises at Emory owes its inspiration to George Peddy Cuttino—Oxonian, distinguished professor of medieval history, and chief marshal of the university from 1977 to 1984.

Emory's first African American graduates—Verdelle Bellamy and Allie Saxon—earned their master's degrees from the Nell Hodgson Woodruff School of Nursing in December 1963, then marched in Commencement the following June. Shown here in the procession, Saxon looks directly at the camera, while Bellamy marches with eyes forward.

CHAPTER 9

Beyond the Quad

HENRY HORNBOSTEL's elegant campus plan for the new university in Druid Hills fit neatly into the seventy-five acres designated for the site. The original campus boundaries began where the Haygood-Hopkins Gate now stands, then extended east along North Decatur Road to Clifton Road, turned left and went north along Clifton almost to the railroad, then turned west to the current McDonough Field before finally turning south and back to the starting point. Taking advantage of the topography of this parcel of land, Hornbostel laid out an academic village on the central hill. On another hill, to the north, across a ravine spanned by a bridge, he situated the hub of social life, including residence halls, dining facilities, assembly buildings, and athletics fields.

The university remained fairly true to that plan until the 1950s, when two academic buildings—now called the Anthropology Building and Tarbutton Hall—went up on the north side of the ravine, and residence halls now called the Complex went up to the south. In subsequent decades, the university not only grew into 750 acres but also began to depart from the elements of Hornbostel's design—the red-tile roofs, the marble cladding, and the tall windows and doorways with Roman arches. Still, despite the intrusion of different architectural styles and the interruption of Hornbostel's patterns for pedestrian and vehicular traffic, his vision for those central seventy-five acres of the original campus continued to guide the development of institutional life into the twenty-first century.

An architectural gem designed by the Atlanta firm Ivey and Crook, the first campus auditorium and dining hall, shown here, filled an essential need at the time of its construction in 1927. It replaced a wooden structure that had burned in 1925. After World War II, the university built an expansion onto the eastern side of the building and renamed it the Alumni Memorial University Center (AMUC) to honor Emory graduates who had fallen in the two world wars. Later, plaques would honor those who gave their lives in Korea and Vietnam. The 1950 expansion, with its arched entrance, is just visible to the right through the trees in this photo. When the Dobbs University Center (DUC) was constructed in 1985–1986, architect John Portman incorporated the 1927 facade into the building as one wall of an atrium called the Coca-Cola Commons. With the demolition of the DUC in 2017 and construction of the new Campus Life Center, the AMUC was restored to full glory as a freestanding structure separated from the Campus Life Center by a green courtyard.

This photo, from the estate of Gardner B. Allen, shows students, faculty, and administrators gathered on the steps of the 1927 Assembly Hall during Junior College Day, May 1930. The day apparently offered an opportunity for students from Emory's two-year colleges in Oxford and Valdosta to get a taste of life at the big-city campus, where they could continue in their junior and senior years. Kneeling in front are, left to right, President Harvey Cox, holding the hand of a little girl; Comer Woodward, dean of Emory-at-Oxford; William B. Stubbs 1919c, dean of Emory-at-Valdosta; Goodrich White 1908c, dean of Emory College; and Theodore Jack, dean of the Graduate School. The children are unidentified. Stubbs, a Rhodes Scholar from Emory, had practiced law in Savannah before becoming the founding dean of the new junior college Emory established in Valdosta in 1928.

During renovation of Glenn Memorial in the fall of 1961, the AMUC served as temporary worship space for the Methodist congregation. In the 1980s, the room shown here would become the Mary Gray Munroe Theater, home to countless productions by Theater Emory.

A hangout for students, Dooley's Den occupied the bottom floor of the AMUC in the 1950s (long before Emory became a tobacco-free campus, as evident by the smokers in the photograph). Later the den would move to Cox Hall, and still later to the Depot. The back of this photo in the archives notes that, in addition to the snack bar, Dooley's Den "contains a piano, record player, television set, and billiard tables" (box 45, folder 11, Emory University Photograph Collection).

From church services to dances to musical soirees, the large interior of the AMUC hosted a wide range of activities, including what might have been Dooley's Ball, shown here, sometime in the 1970s.

Built in 1960 and named for Harvey Warren Cox, Emory's longest-serving president, Cox Hall was renovated in 1980 and again in 1993. The 1993 renovation turned the second-floor cafeteria into a student computing center, moved the food court to the lower level, and added a clock tower to the exterior. In 2000, trustee emeritus William Robinson and his wife, Betty, donated a set of bells to play the Westminster Chimes every quarter hour and an electronic carillon and speaker system capable of playing recorded music, including the alma mater at noon and 6:00 p.m. daily. At some point, students suggested that the evening rendition should occur at 6:36—in military time, 18:36, commemorating the year of Emory's founding.

Because the 1993 renovation eliminated the cafeteria that had been used by hospital employees and visitors as well as by students, the Emory University Hospital built a new cafeteria behind its G Wing. The contractor for the hospital cafeteria set up a command post in a trailer across Asbury Circle, near Candler Library, and outside the trailer stood a soft-drink vending machine—for Pepsi. By midmorning, after a call from the President's Office, that vending machine had been replaced by one for Coca-Cola.

Until the 1993 renovation of Cox Hall, the large cafeteria on the second floor served both the university and visitors to Emory University Hospital next door.

Part of the unprecedented and still never duplicated building fury after World War II, the Geology Building (left) and Biology Building (right) appear in the distance near Dobbs Hall, to the left. Completed in 1951, Geology and Biology were renovated in 1992–1993 and renamed. Geology is now the Anthropology Building, and Biology is now Ben J. Tarbutton Hall, named for a 1905 graduate of the college by his son Ben J. Tarbutton Jr. 1949OX 1951C, who served many years as a trustee. Today the George W. Woodruff Physical Education Center rises to the left of this perspective, but the field in front still serves as the soccer pitch and athletic track.

Built in 1916 by the Seaboard Coast Line Railroad to accommodate passengers to and from the new university being built in Druid Hills, this depot originally bore the place name "Emory, GA." Until 1969, travelers could catch the Silver Comet here and ride it to New York City, and passenger service connected Emory to other parts of Georgia. (Flannery O'Connor mentions the Emory station in one of her short stories, when the conductor calls out the stop at "MMMRY.") During the 1970s, after the railroad stopped both passenger service and freight deliveries to the station, the Emory Employees Federal Credit Union leased the depot, known for many years as the old Seaboard Coast Line Railroad station. The credit union left in 1981, and the university converted the space for use as a restaurant. Administrators considered opening a campus pub here, but state law prohibited sale of alcoholic beverages on campuses. Instead, a new dining facility, the Depot, opened in February 1982, and the place has undergone many changes in name, menu, and decor ever since.

In 1947 the name of the station was changed from "Emory, GA," to "Emory University, GA." In fact, the postal address for Emory in Druid Hills remained Emory University, Georgia, until 1958, despite frequent attempts by the university to associate postally with the city of Atlanta. At last, on May 1 of that year, according to historian Thomas H. English, the university's address became Atlanta 22, subsequently changed to Atlanta 30322 with the introduction of zip codes (English, *Emory University, 1915–1965*, 102).

No documentation exists to indicate why Marshal Ferdinand Foch, the commander-in-chief of Allied forces in the last months of World War I, had a hero's welcome at the Emory depot on December 9, 1921. He may have come to Atlanta to visit Pershing Point, the small park in Midtown named in 1918 to honor General John Pershing, commander of the American Expeditionary Forces, and graced in 1920 with a plaque honoring Fulton County men who had died in the war. Whatever the reason, Marshal Foch's stop at Emory called for ample bunting, and many of the men in uniform likely were Emory ROTC students and their instructors. Emory, in fact, had made a special contribution to the war effort, when physicians teaching in the Emory medical school and nurses from Wesley Memorial Hospital (later Emory University Hospital) joined others from Atlanta to form the Emory Unit, as it was named. Establishing Base Hospital 43, they served the wounded and ill near the battlefields of France from June 1918 to January 1919. The unit was reactivated during World War II to serve in North Africa and France.

Arthur Tufts.

THE ENCHANTED WOODLAND
OF ARTHUR TUFTS

Arthur Tufts, the trusted contractor recommended by Asa Candler and builder of the Candler Building in New York City, the Candler Building in Atlanta, and many other magnificent structures, oversaw early construction of the Druid Hills campus.

In 1916 Tufts built his house just off Clifton Road and called it Woodland. The driveway had two gates—an "upper gate" at the northern end of his property, and a "lower gate" at the southern end—names that still survive in Uppergate Drive and the Lowergate parking decks. From this proximity to the campus, Tufts supervised the construction of Emory until his death from pneumonia at the age of forty-one in 1920. His widow, Jeanie Tufts, continued living there until

Arthur Tufts's house, Woodland, circa 1920.

Arthur Tufts's garden now sprouts a parking deck behind the Emory Clinic.

Woodland still stands along Uppergate Drive.

1940. Renamed Uppergate House, the concrete structure served as the home of the university computing center and the Biomedical Data Processing and Analysis Center in the late 1960s and early 1970s.

A former director of the computing center has told the story of working alone in the house late at night when a ghostly woman appeared out of nowhere and made the hair on his neck stand up. Mike Wilhoit had finished rewiring a circuit in the basement and had made his way to the main computer room—unlocking and relocking doors along the way—when he encountered the shape of a woman. She asked him calmly if her son was there—and then, just as quietly, disappeared, while Wilhoit stood shaking and wondering how she had gotten into the building. Was this Jeanie Tufts, the real-life widow of Arthur Tufts, somehow showing up unexpectedly three decades after moving out of the house? It's possible but unlikely. Jeanie Tufts was eighty-seven years old and infirm at the time. She died four years later.

Edgar H. Johnson 1891c, longtime professor of political science and economics at Emory during its Oxford days, served as dean of Emory College from 1915 until the college moved to Atlanta in 1919. He saw the transition as an opportunity to tap into the growing national interest in schools for business in the early decades of the twentieth century, and he recommended establishing an undergraduate business program. The trustees agreed, and in 1919 the School of Business Administration took up residence in the basement of the Law School Building (now Carlos Hall). There the school remained until after World War II. At last, needing space during the postwar boom, the school gained new quarters in 1947 thanks to a gift from the Rich Foundation in memory of Morris, Daniel, and Emanuel Rich, the founders of Rich's department store in Atlanta (later acquired by Macy's). Within a few decades, the school again had outgrown its space; it moved in 1997 to its new home on Clifton Road and took a new name, the Goizueta Business School. The Rich Building became home to the departments of dance, film studies, theater, and economics.

As early as the mid-1950s, the dean of the law school was complaining to the university administration about the inadequacy of the school's original building on the Quad, where the school had opened in 1916. The un-air-conditioned building made evening courses in the summer unbearable, the library was cramped, classrooms were too small, and enrollment demanded more and better space. E. Smythe Gambrell, an eminent Atlanta attorney with a Harvard law degree, former president of the American Bar Association, and one of the first faculty members at Emory Law, stepped forward to make a lead gift for a new building, named for his parents. This photo shows Gambrell Hall under construction in 1973.

OPPOSITE: Gambrell Hall, early 1970s.

Ambitiously aiming to raise what was then a magnificent sum of $10 million in ten years, Emory in 1926 launched a campaign intended to endow professorships and pay for new buildings. One of these buildings would be a fine arts center and performance space. Sunk by the beginning of the Great Depression three years later, the fundraising campaign raised less than a fifth of its goal. To fill the gap left by the unbuilt arts center, Charles Howard Candler Sr. and his wife, Flora Glenn Candler, gave the money to build Glenn Memorial. For decades, the auditorium served a dual function as an acoustically superb concert hall and as the beautifully appointed worship space for the Methodist congregation that had grown up on the campus. Not until 2003, with the dedication of the Donna and Marvin Schwartz Center for Performing Arts, would the university achieve its 1926 goal of a separate arts center. Meanwhile, Glenn hosted concerts by artists such as Bob Dylan, Cecilia Bartoli, and Chick Corea, as well as the annual Festival of Nine Lessons and Carols for Christmas. This photo shows the streetcar that ran down North Decatur Road past Glenn Memorial until 1947.

This photo of Eleanor Roosevelt speaking at Glenn Memorial on February 26, 1960, shows the original proscenium design with columns on either side of the stage. Renovation of the auditorium the following year removed those columns and reconfigured the stage to create the large chancel that currently exists. Roosevelt was on campus to speak as part of a three-day conference on world affairs sponsored by the International Relations Club of Emory. She is flanked by vice president and dean of the faculties Judson C. Ward 1933C 1934G to her right and *Atlanta Constitution* editor Ralph McGill to her left.

Dedicated in 1937, the Haygood-Hopkins Gate pays tribute to two nineteenth-century Emory presidents who had an enduring impact not only on the college but on higher education well beyond their alma mater. Atticus Greene Haygood and Isaac Stiles Hopkins were 1859 classmates at Emory, and while both entered the Methodist ministry, they ended up together on the faculty in Oxford. Haygood later helped build historically black colleges in the South and served as a Methodist bishop, while Hopkins went on to become the founding president of Georgia Tech.

The gate not only provides a passageway into the Druid Hills campus but also harks back to that original campus in Oxford. Symbolically, the iconic arch welcomes the world in and identifies this place as distinctively Emory through the name under the emblematic lamp of learning. The gate also serves as a reminder of some of Emory's institutional values. Words from Haygood's famous "New South" sermon are chiseled into his pillar, on the left: "Let us stand by what is good and try to make it better." (This quotation also greets visitors at the entrance to the Oxford campus.) The gate was the gift of alumnus Linton Robeson 1886c to memorialize the men who had presided over Emory during his student days.

The center of business activity in Druid Hills from the beginning, Emory Village once thrived with twice as many storefronts as it has now. Shown in this photo, taken in the 1940s, the shopping strip to the left of the Gulf truck included a cinema. A fire in 1979 destroyed most of that wing.

Sleek 1940s-vintage automobiles nosed into tight parking spaces in front of the Emory Village shops stretching downhill from the Emory campus.

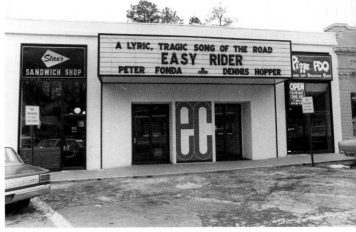

The Emory Cinema would not be riding easy much longer, as a fire begun in the kitchen of a nearby eatery on January 2, 1979, burned out six or seven of the neighboring shops, including this movie theater and the Emory bookstore. The blaze made room for a parking lot, and the few businesses untouched by the flames would become restaurants in the coming decades. Fortunately, the conflagration spared Everybody's Pizza, a favorite haunt of Emory people for forty-one years before closing in 2013.

CHAPTER 10

Libraries

THE MOVE OF Emory College from Oxford to Druid Hills in 1919 also led to the creation of two new schools of the university—the Graduate School and the School of Business Administration, later named the Goizueta Business School. Over the next seven years, the university packed the library resources for all of these new schools into the basement of the Old Theology Building, whose first floor also contained the library for the theology school. Finally, in 1924, Asa Candler, still chair of the board of trustees and a profoundly generous benefactor to the school, gave $400,000 to build a new library. He was present at the ground breaking but was too ill to attend the dedication in February 1926. The library provided greater capacity not only for the arts and sciences library materials but also for administrative offices, which moved out of the second floor of the Physics Building and into the first two floors of the library.

The establishment of Emory University just six miles from the heart of Atlanta also opened the way for several older schools to merge with the new university. One of these was a library school, begun as an apprentice training program when the Carnegie Library opened in downtown Atlanta in 1899. The program later expanded into the Carnegie Library Training School of Atlanta. Under the direction of Tommie Dora Barker—an alumna of the school and the first woman to receive an honorary degree from Emory (in 1930)—the school merged with Emory in 1925 and moved to the Asa Griggs Candler Library in 1930. There it stayed until 1988, changing its name along the way to the Graduate Division of Library and Information Sciences. By the 1980s, technology, economics, and new interdisciplinary approaches to librarianship had dramatically changed the field. The trustees and administration determined that

The Asa Griggs Candler Library sometime in the decade after its 1926 construction. The Old Theology Building stands in the distance across the Quad.

Asa Griggs Candler Sr., the aging benefactor and, arguably, founder of Emory University in its Atlanta location, helped break ground on February 10, 1925, for the library that bears his name. Clearly frail in this photo, he lived on until March 1929, having guided Emory's fortunes for twenty-three years as chair of the board since the college's days in Oxford.

too great an investment would be needed to bring the division into the first rank of library schools in the United States, and the university phased out the division. Emory awarded its last library science degrees in 1988.

Less than three decades after the opening of Candler Library, the building was ready to burst. Some relief came in 1955, when a gift from board chair Charles Howard Candler Sr. 1898C 1902M made possible the construction of the Administration Building at the opposite end of the Quadrangle. Even with the move of administrative offices from the library into the new building, however, the growing collections in Candler required more shelf space. Pressed for money, in 1957 the trustees authorized cutting the beautiful two-story-high reading room in half, horizontally, to add another floor of book stacks. The building served in that chopped-up condition for another half century. Finally, the turn of the millennium became the right time to restore this gem at the eastern end of the Quadrangle. Contractors gutted the building and reconstructed it along the lines of its original blueprints, with the addition of a

The faculty, staff, and students of the library school in front of Candler Library in 1931.

Students—many of them GIs back from the war—line up to register in Candler Library, September 30, 1946.

This photo shows the Candler Library service desk around 1950.

ten-thousand-square-foot bump out on the eastern side to provide access from Asbury Circle for the first time. The $17 million rejuvenated beauty reopened in 2004.

The decision by the university to begin offering PhD degrees in the late 1940s meant that Emory now had to build a real research library. As the 1960s dawned, it was clear that Candler Library, already inadequate despite the addition of stack space in its 1957 renovation, would never do. Library director Guy Lyle oversaw planning for a new, ten-story tower. Situated near the library named for Asa Candler, the most generous benefactor of the university in the first half of the twentieth century, the new library bears the name of Robert W. Woodruff, the most generous benefactor in the second half of that century. Both men became fabulously wealthy by their respective decades-long leadership of the Coca-Cola Company.

The new library served the needs of scholars but had several negative impacts on the campus, including blocking off Kilgo

Robert W. Woodruff Library, 1969.

Built in 1995 as the Center for Library and Information Resources (CLAIR), the round addition between Candler Library on the left and Woodruff Library on the right now is simply regarded as part of Woodruff. Fittingly, an elevated and enclosed bridge between Candler and Woodruff symbolizes a bridge between the first half of the twentieth century and the second half, the respective eras when these two leaders of the Coca-Cola Company, Asa Griggs Candler and Robert W. Woodruff, also held sway as the principal benefactors of the university.

Circle where the roadway rounded the southeastern corners of the History Building (now Bowden Hall) and Candler Library. As a result, the road no longer completely encircled the Quadrangle. (The circle would be plugged again at its northwest corner when White Hall was built in 1977). The new library also rose out of the heavily wooded ravine that had separated the Quadrangle from the C. L. Fishburne Building. A ramp sloped up toward the library's surrounding plaza and entrance over the stream that flows into Baker Woodlands (Antoinette Candler Creek). That ramp was demolished in the 1990s as a new center for digital resources, teaching facilities, and library services was added to the northern side of Woodruff Library.

Among all the facilities on American college and university campuses, maybe none has experienced such extraordinary transformation over the last thirty years as the libraries. Where students once roamed between immovable stacks of books reaching from floor to ceiling, movable compact shelving now often doubles the number of volumes housed in a given space. Where ranks of study desks graced by lamps once filled reading rooms for use by solitary scholars, clusters of work stations now invite students to collaborate around the latest large-screen desktop computers. Reference librarians are as likely to refer scholars to a website as to reach for a book on a shelf. Most amazing of all, in spaces where food and liquids once were viewed with the same forbidding countenance that customs officials reserve for contraband, libraries now frequently include a coffee shop and snack bar to help fuel the scholarly enterprise. Maybe no other buildings on campus so perfectly epitomize the Emory mission to "create, preserve, teach, and apply knowledge in service of humanity"—and in service of students, faculty, and staff alike.

CHAPTER 11

Living on Campus

FEW SPACES mold students' perception of the campus as a place more indelibly than the spaces where they hang their clothes. Residence halls—what earlier generations called dormitories—offer many students their first experience of living in complete, grown-up independence. Some students later move into fraternity houses or sorority lodges or opt to live off campus. Yet those first semesters spent sleeping, studying, and brushing teeth in sometimes Spartan, sometimes elegant campus housing are also the months when life-long friendships take root.

In a sense, the residence hall is the essential setting where the drama of college life begins to unfold. Yes, the classroom and laboratory are critical to thought, the library and archives foster learning, the athletic field and court nurture comradeship and team spirit—but the residence hall harbors the most personal moments. This is where students experience deep self-doubt in the quiet of the night or share high hopes with roommates and friends. It is the arena of tomfoolery and, unfortunately, drunkenness, of late-night bull sessions and the negotiation of intimate favors.

At Emory, "the hall" serves as the focal point for orienting first-year students. At Songfest, marking the end of orientation, first-year students organized by hall perform original tunes to sing the praises of their new habitats. The winning hall has bragging rights for eternity, and alumni don't forget if their hall won Songfest. Residence halls are also the scene of faculty "last lectures" and thematic extracurricular exploration of environmental stewardship, civic engagement, or leadership. The place of residence lingers in memory of alumni as a place that either hones survival skills or offers nurturing. While the rooms of newer halls are more commodious than earlier

Samuel Candler Dobbs Hall appears here behind the men and women attending the 1920 Coca-Cola convention, held on the Emory campus when the hall's namesake was president of the Coca-Cola Company. One of two residence halls built for the opening of the Druid Hills campus in 1916, Dobbs Hall honors the trustee who gave the money for its construction. Dobbs was a nephew of Asa Griggs Candler Sr. and served as president of Coca-Cola from 1919 to 1922.

For its first three years, until Emory College moved to Atlanta, this building housed only students in the schools of theology, law, and medicine. The late Nolan Bailey Harmon, longtime Methodist bishop and a trustee of the university, recounted his time living in Dobbs Hall during his first year as a student in the theology school. According to Harmon's perhaps apocryphal story, not all the doors yet had latches when he moved in, and wind through the open windows on a sultry September night kept the doors swinging and banging, keeping young Harmon from sleep. The hall continues in use as a residence for first-year students in Emory College.

In 1962 the university renovated Dobbs Hall and added an extension to the back. This photo shows the back of Dobbs perhaps in the 1940s. The street to the left was Arkwright Drive and is now a sidewalk between Dobbs and the George W. Woodruff Physical Education Center and soccer field.

Winship Hall stood almost directly across the street from Dobbs Hall and, like its partner dormitory, served professional-school students when it opened in 1916. Its basement would later become an exercise room, one of the first gymnasium spaces on the Atlanta campus. The building's namesake, George Winship, had built an extraordinarily successful career in manufacturing and cotton and had served as an Emory trustee. He died at the age of eighty-one in April 1916, just months before the opening of the dormitory that would bear his name. The building was razed in the early 1980s to make way for the Dobbs University Center (DUC), named for R. Howard Dobbs, an Emory trustee and no relation to Samuel Candler Dobbs. The Winship Ballroom in the DUC continued to honor Winship's legacy until the DUC was razed in 2017 to make way for the new Campus Life Center.

dorm rooms, and buildings have been fitted for air-conditioning and Wi-Fi, the emotional life lived in these spaces has probably changed little since residence halls first appeared at Emory.

A STORY OF SPECIAL ACCOMMODATION

Joel Geffen 1922C and Louis Geffen 1923C were two of the first Jewish students to attend Emory. (Joel Geffen is listed incorrectly in the 1926 alumni directory as Joseph Geffen.) Their father, Rabbi Tobias Geffen (1870–1970), the leading Orthodox rabbi in the Southeast, served Congregation Shearith Israel in Atlanta for decades. Four of the rabbi's sons and two of his daughters earned a total of eight degrees from Emory, as at least one of them was enrolled from 1919 to 1927.

According to family lore, Rabbi Geffen consulted with Chancellor Warren Candler out of concern about possible barriers to his sons' academic progress. At the time, Saturday morning classes were

This undated photo of Alabama Hall may have been taken during the 1920s, when Dobbs and Winship Halls also were photographed. Built in 1919, Alabama Hall was named for the Alabama Conference of the Methodist Episcopal Church, South, which had raised most of the funds to construct the building.

Louis Geffen 1923c in front of Alabama Hall.

Louis Geffen's parents, Rabbi Tobias and Sara Geffen, in front of Alabama Hall.

mandatory and Saturday exams were common. As observant Orthodox Jews, Joel and Louis risked being unfairly burdened by exams on the Sabbath. The rabbi asked if they could receive some accommodation. Indeed, yes, answered Bishop Candler.

A letter from the B'nai B'rith director to President Harvey Cox in the 1930s goes further in the story. Whether true or not, the story recounts that when Candler, the bishop chancellor, resided at 1655 North Decatur Road, he offered to let several Jewish students—perhaps one or two of them Geffens—stay at his home on Friday nights. The bishop's house, now owned by Emory, still stands almost directly across from the entrance to Fishburne parking deck. (Through the decades, the building has housed various university offices.) From there the short walk across the street to the campus posed no difficulties.

NAMING THE HALLS

The first buildings on the Atlanta campus to bear the names of Emory presidents from the old Oxford days were Longstreet Hall and Means Hall, dedicated in 1955 during the great boom of the postwar decade and subsequently often referred to as Longstreet-Means Hall. Augustus Baldwin Longstreet—lawyer, minister, journalist, and fiction writer (inducted into the Georgia Writers Hall of Fame)—served as Emory's second president, from 1840 to 1848. Longstreet had made his fortune as well as his fame with his book *Georgia Scenes*, a collection of humorous sketches about rural and small-town life, and he used his personal wealth to help keep the college afloat. When he left the presidency, he wrote off the substantial funds he had lent the college. Alexander Means—scientist, minister, physician, and poet—served on the faculty for many years and briefly (1854–1855) as president of the college before deciding to devote his energies to teaching in the Atlanta Medical College and the Augusta Medical College. Fascinated by the potential for electricity, he is reputed to have demonstrated an incandescent light as early as 1850.

Both Longstreet and Means, like every other antebellum president and trustee of Emory College, were slave owners, and the naming of the buildings for them in 1955, the year after the U.S. Supreme Court decided the case of *Brown v. Board of Education of Topeka, Kansas*, leads to speculation about the purpose of the naming. In 1956, one year after the dedication of Longstreet-Means, the Georgia legislature changed the design of the state flag to incorporate the Confederate battle emblem. Throughout the South in the 1950s, schools, buildings, streets, and highways were named for Confederate leaders, ostensibly to honor southern "heritage" but implicitly to resist federal mandates for integration.

No evidence exists that the Emory board of trustees was motivated by resistance to civil rights or by pride in Confederate heritage in naming two new dormitories. The January 20, 1955, Executive Committee resolution naming the halls refers to Longstreet as "a widely known writer and minister who was President of Emory College at Oxford" and refers to Means as "a minister and perhaps best known for his research in the field of electricity, who was President of Emory College." Three years after the opening of Longstreet-Means, the university built Thomas, Hopkins, and Smith Halls (The Complex), named for one Emory president (James R. Thomas) who served before and after the Civil War and for two (Isaac Stiles Hopkins and Luther M. Smith) who served after the war. These five halls together appear to have served as a way of remembering on the Druid Hills campus the history of Emory College from its days in Oxford. Similarly, names of streets on the Druid Hills campus—Pierce Drive, Dowman Drive, Dickey Drive—all

The original
Longstreet-Means
Hall, 1955.

honor Emory presidents who served while Emory College was in Oxford.

As part of an effort to create a greater sense of coherence among first-year Emory College students, the university in the early 2000s began to build a "freshman village" around the corner of Asbury Circle and Eagle Row. Old dormitories (Longstreet-Means, Trimble, and McTyeire, along with the J. Pollard Turman Residential Center next to Druid Hills High School) came down, while larger, somewhat luxurious residence halls went up. Most of the new buildings bore the names of Emory "firsts"—Ignatius Few Hall for the first president of the college, Lettie Pate Evans Hall for the first female trustee, Eléonore Raoul Hall for the first woman to enroll in the university, and Hamilton Holmes Hall for the first African American graduate of the medical school. The current Longstreet-Means Hall was dedicated in 2010. Its name and that of Turman Hall depart from others in the freshman village in not recognizing a first. The perpetuation of Longstreet-Means and Turman was intended to recognize the affiliation of decades of alumni who had lived in the older halls.

By the time the university trustees voted in 1953 to admit women as residential students, more than two hundred women already had received bachelor's degrees from Emory College, and many more had earned degrees from the graduate and professional schools. Still, the only campus housing for women until then had been Harris Hall, built for nursing students in 1929. Not until 1958 did the university provide sufficient housing for women who wanted to live on campus.

With those new residence halls under construction in 1958, the director of housing suggested that since the new dorms would house women, perhaps they should bear women's names. Two names he suggested were those of Flora Glenn Candler, a generous patron of the arts and the wife of the late board chair Charles Howard Candler Sr.; and Nell Hodgson Woodruff, wife of Coca-Cola magnate Robert W. Woodruff. Others suggested naming the dorms for the wives of prominent trustees or faculty members, or for nursing administrators, or for professors from the Oxford days of Emory College, or even for Emmie Stewart, Sallie Stewart, and Lynn Branham—women who had run popular boarding houses for students in Oxford.

Before the opening of the Complex in the fall of 1958, Bradford D. Ansley, director of development and public relations, suggested that the precedent of Longstreet-Means Hall pointed to naming the new halls for presidents who had served at Oxford. And so it was done: the buildings bear the names of James R. Thomas, Luther M. Smith, and Isaac Stiles Hopkins, although no signage indicates which building is which.

The Complex—Thomas, Smith, and Hopkins Halls. The original caption of this photo, provided to media by Emory in January 1959, reads, "Emory coeds line up on balconies of striking new dormitories."

In 1922, when Wesley Memorial Hospital moved from its original home in downtown Atlanta to new quarters on Clifton Road, it brought with it the nurses training program that had been established with the hospital in 1905. Within a few years after the move, the nurses program had outgrown space available in the hospital, and in 1929 the children of Asa Griggs Candler Sr. paid for a new building to house the growing cadre of nursing students. Designed by Atlanta architect Philip Trammell Shutze and named for Florence Candler Harris (the older sister of Asa Sr.), Harris Hall joins ten other buildings on the Druid Hills campus listed on the National Register of Historic Places. The others are Old Theology, Carlos Hall, Callaway North, Callaway South, Asa Candler Library, Glenn Memorial, the Church School Building, Dobbs Hall, the 1922 Emory Hospital, and Uppergate House (the Tufts House, originally named Woodland).

Overcrowded residence halls and inadequate housing for married students led the
university to bring a hundred trailers to campus and park them at the present site
of Longstreet-Means Hall and the James B. Williams Medical Education Building.
Married couples—some of them with very young children—lived in these
un-air-conditioned trailers, which were a fixture of the campus from February 1946
to September 1952. Emory historian Thomas H. English asserts that "the young
people who began family life in [Trailertown's] straitened bounds gave every
appearance of savoring the experience" (English, *Emory University 1915–1965*, 65–66).
The building in the background is Winship Hall.

While the Oxford campus had a relatively modern, new gymnasium early in the twentieth century, athletic facilities on the Druid Hills campus took time to develop. The first gym in Druid Hills was a basement room in Winship Hall outfitted with medicine balls, barbells, and mats. A small building erected in the 1920s near the current WaterHub served for the next two decades. After World War II, however, the need for a real gymnasium was evident. The innovative business manager of the university bought an unused airplane hangar in Oklahoma and had it shipped to the campus, where it served as the frame for the new Field House.

One of the rites of passage for first-year students, from 1923 until its prohibition in 1955, was pushball. Popular on many campuses in the first half of the twentieth century, the game at Emory pitted freshmen against sophomores. If the freshmen won, they were allowed to forgo wearing rat caps and other practices that nowadays would amount to hazing (for example, having to wear their shirts, ties, and coats backward, having to walk up stairs and through doorways backward, and addressing older students with a bow and a doff of their caps). Never well refereed or even played according to the rules, the games always concluded with the depantsing of the refs, who were tossed into a creek near the playing field. These descents into free-for-alls led to so many injuries that the administration banned the game after the 1955 contest.

CHAPTER 12

The Bridges of Emory Campus

When Henry Hornbostel designed the Druid Hills campus, he created a serene entrance that wound through woods until opening onto a vista of academic buildings. Perhaps he was inspired by the work of Frederick Law Olmsted and his sons, who had planned the neighborhood of Druid Hills and who had created the impressive landscape architecture of Biltmore, the estate of George Washington Vanderbilt II in Asheville, North Carolina. The original approach to the university buildings from Emory Village must have given the impression of entering a country estate.

Taking advantage of the topography, Hornbostel spanned the ravines and two major streams of the campus's seventy-five acres with single-arch bridges, whose elegant guardrails belie their concrete construction. The driveway entering the campus from North Decatur Road cut through woods—between what is now the Baker Woodlands to the left and Glenn Memorial to the right. Crossing the first of three large, concrete bridges, the road then turned left at about where the Rich Building now stands, then crossed a second bridge, now called the Mizell Bridge, which still spans Antoinette Candler Creek behind the Michael C. Carlos Museum.

Until the construction of Woodruff Library, traffic flowed across the Mizell Bridge toward the Quadrangle and turned right, toward Candler Library. Later, when Woodruff Library blocked the road, arrows directed vehicles to the left, toward the Administration Building. Still later, traffic would be directed in the opposite direction, away from the Quad toward the Rich Building.

Hornbostel's third elegant bridge spanned a second ravine and creek (Hornbostel Creek) and connected the academic Quadrangle area to the dormitories and athletics spaces. In 1960 the ravine on

the east side of the bridge would be filled in with the construction of Cox Hall. Five decades further on, weekly farmers markets
would line the bridge with locally grown and prepared foods, as the
university brought greater food awareness to its emphasis on environmental, social, and economic sustainability.

Less impressive but functionally necessary bridges elsewhere
on campus helped pedestrians navigate the hills and valleys of the
Emory terrain. One such bridge linked two segments of a path that
led through the woods from the south end of Candler Library and up
the hill toward the C. L. Fishburne Building, where the Educational
Studies Division had its home for many decades. The span crossed
high over Antoinette Candler Creek. By 1969 this bridge had been
removed, and the spot was filled in by the new Robert W. Woodruff
Library. A steel conduit directed the flow of the creek under a ramp
leading up to the library.

Since the early 1990s, Emory has built additional bridges to make
the flow of pedestrians and vehicles more manageable. A massive
concrete bridge, built for $1 million in the early 1990s and bearing
the Emory shield stamped into its balustrades, has one foot planted

The original entrance
to the Druid Hills
campus crossed this
bridge over a gully,
which was filled in
sometime in the late
1940s.

Pedestrians and drivers approached the Quadrangle over a second bridge across the stream through Baker Woodlands. This view onto the Quad is now blocked by the Michael C. Carlos Museum.

near the current Longstreet-Means Hall, from which it rises over Asbury Circle and the Depot to straddle the CSX railroad and step with its other foot beside the Whitehead Research Building. Until the construction of this bridge, pedestrians had to make their way the extra hundred yards to Clifton Road, where a narrow sidewalk abutted the busy street and made the crowded pavement risky. Later, when the Miller-Ward Alumni House was completed in 2000, the university erected an iron bridge so pedestrians could easily cross Houston Mill Road from the Emory Conference Center Hotel to the alumni house and back. The latest addition to the bridge constellation is a suspension bridge for pedestrians to cross the South Fork of Peachtree Creek not far from Lullwater House, making it easier for Emory physicians to walk from the VA Hospital to the main campus and for weekend walkers to explore the full environs of Lullwater.

This photo, taken around 1960, shows one-way traffic across the Mizell Bridge approaching the Quadrangle. After construction of the Michael C. Carlos Museum, the one-way bridge reversed direction.

Cox Hall bridge, 1930s. Note the water tower in the background,
erected in 1933 and removed in 2007; see page 200.

The view in this photo, taken around 1946, looks toward the Quadrangle, with Candler Library
to the left and the Physics and Chemistry Buildings (now the Callaway Center) to the right.

The perspective here shows the same pedestrian bridge from the vantage of the stream that flows through the ravine, Antoinette Candler Creek.

Fishburne path bridge, long vanished. William Dillingham 1955C 1956G, the Charles Howard Candler Professor of American Literature, Emeritus, once remarked, "When I came to Emory, it was a small school in a forest." This photo may have been taken about the time Dillingham arrived at Emory in 1951.

CHAPTER 13

The Long and Dangerous Journey

THE VERY FIRST graduate course I enrolled in at Emory, in the fall of 1983, was worth a mere single credit. It was not the only course I was taking that semester, but it was first on the schedule, so I think of it as my toe dip into the frigid waters of the PhD. I was enrolled in the doctoral program in ethics and society in the Graduate Division of Religion. My heart in many ways, though, was invested in the study of religion and literature. I had just finished a divinity degree the previous spring, and a few years before that had earned a master's degree in literature, and the marriage of these two disciplines attracted me as much as the study of how morality arose out of social arrangements and institutions. Thus, my escape to the one-credit seminar on the religious dimensions of literature.

A small band of like-minded students gathered weekly that fall in a seminar room on the second floor of what was then called the Physics Building—now the Callaway Center South. The physicists had decamped many years before for quarters elsewhere, leaving the 1919 structure with its original name chiseled into a concrete decorative tablet over the front entrance and attached in large black metal letters to the facade next to the doorway. The Religion Department and the Institute of the Liberal Arts now occupied the building. To suggest the nature of the scholarship that now filled the place, some wag had spray-painted the word "META" to the left of the word "PHYSICS."

Our particular interest that semester was certainly metaphysical—a close reading of *The Symbolism of Evil* by Paul Ricoeur. At the head of the table, guiding our examination of the matter, sat a bearded, quizzical, and brilliant fifty-three-year-old professor named David H. Hesla.

Physics Building before 1993 (now Callaway Center South).

David had earned his PhD studying literature and theology at the University of Chicago and then joined the Emory faculty in 1965, devoting his scholarship to the works of Samuel Beckett. As a teacher, he deployed the Socratic method like an emery board on his students' minds, polishing the best of them and sharpening the weaker. He delighted in his reputation as a curmudgeon, though his gruff demeanor disguised a kindly humor and a genuine concern for his students' well-being, both intellectual and personal.

Not until fifteen years or so after that seminar did I experience David's unique and memorable guided tour of the nonmetaphysical world of the campus. He had been giving this tour for years as a teaching exercise to open his students' minds by opening their eyes. He called it "The Long and Dangerous Journey," and one day I received an email invitation to come along.

Thinking back, trying to retrieve fact from the muddle of memory, I believe we gathered for the journey on a late afternoon in autumn, toward the end of October, when the leaves were mostly gold and red and clouds hung low, a classic moment on a university campus. Or maybe it was in the early spring, when the trees on the Quad were just waking up and the air still held some of the chill of winter. Whichever season it was, David's freshman seminar class of about a dozen students, joined by several hangers-on like me, stood expectantly on the sidewalk in front of the Physics Building. By then in his late sixties, David stepped from the building, said hello, and admonished the assembled learners: "Forget what you think you know about the history, geography, and layout of this place. Ignore what you believe you have experienced of it before. Become a phenomenologist. Look at what is in front of your eyes and ask yourself what you are seeing. And keep up—I do not walk backward like an admissions office tour guide, and I do not walk slowly."

With that, he led the group onto the grass of the Quad and gave a slow turn of 360 degrees, telling his followers to do the same. "Which building," he asked, "is the most important building that you can see? Remember, please, that you do not know their names."

A moment of silence, and then several students offered tentative suggestions: "that one at this end of the Quad" (Candler Library); "that one at the far end" (the Administration Building); "the one in the middle with the stairs going up like a kind of pyramid" (the Michael C. Carlos Museum).

"Why?"

"Well," said one student, "because that one with the pyramid is in the middle of one side of the Quad and looks imposing; it's flanked by two smaller-looking buildings; and, besides, its architecture is different from that of the others."

"Well," said another, "because the building at this end of the Quad has interesting sconces and more steps than the other buildings—five or six leading to a single entrance."

"Ah, well," said another, "that building at the far end facing this way has even more steps and *three* entrances in the front."

And so it went. David did not offer up an answer, but the students were limbering up their imaginations, beginning to get the feel of how to look at things afresh and analyze them without drawing on the familiar and easy habits with which they had once organized the world around them. The Quad had become the New World, a place never seen before, or at least never seen in quite this way.

More questions followed. "Is the Quad masculine or feminine?"

"Well, there's that flagpole," said one student.

"No," said another, "look how the space is shaped like a womb."

To which David added, "What do we call the college that cultivates our minds and our characters? Alma mater—nurturing mother."

David really slipped the exercise into a higher gear while standing in front of Bowden Hall. Pointing to the entrance of the building, he asked again what the students saw.

"A doorway."

"Yes, but what's around it?"

"An arch."

"What kind of arch?"

"One that's curved at the top."

"And do you know what term architects use for that curved arch?"

"A Roman arch?"

"Yes, because this is the kind of arch the Romans used. Do you notice anything else about that doorway?"

"There's another kind of arch set inside the Roman arch—two vertical lines with a triangle on top of them."

"And what do you associate that design with?"

"Greece."

"Yes, exactly—this is the kind of arch you would find at, say, the Parthenon. Does that Greek arch set inside the Roman arch suggest anything else to you?"

Much staring, and then someone giggled.

"What?"

"Well—the Greek arch with the triangle on top looks kind of like . . ."

"Like what?"

"Well, . . . kind of like . . . a penis."

In a moment, everyone saw it, and then they saw what appeared to be a male sex organ inside a female sex organ.

"Yes," said David, "this is Greece 'doing it to' Rome." Although he did not use the term "doing it to." He dropped the f-bomb, surely not the first time the students had heard the word, but probably the first they had heard it from the lips of a senior faculty member in the hallowed space of the Quadrangle.

Later the group would stand near the southeast corner of Cannon Chapel, where a ramp leads up from the Quad to the chapel's heavy wooden doors. From that spot the students could see the horizontal lines of two barrel vaults of the roof covering the chapel, one long barrel rising behind the other, and both of them stretching from the cubelike eastern end of the building on the students' right to the rounded western end on the left, where a flat, straight steeple with a cross rose above the vaults.

"Do you see a resemblance to anything?" Eventually someone would see that the building from that angle looked a bit like an old steam locomotive. David would remind the group that Atlanta began life as a place called Terminus, the end of the railroad line. Perhaps, he suggested, this was architect Paul Rudolph's subtle homage to the hometown of the university.

Leading the group inside the building to the sanctuary, David pointed out how the seating was arranged in a rising spiral of sections. From the floor, a bank of pews sloped up and back toward the south wall, and then to the left, up a few steps, another bank of pews stretched along the eastern wall, overlooking the sanctuary below as if from a balcony. Then, moving left once again, the seating stepped up toward a still higher bank of pews along the northern wall, giving persons seated there an even higher perch from which to survey all below. Finally, behind the organ in the northwest corner, another few steps led up to the highest bank of pews along the western wall, where the seats peered from thirty feet above the floor.

For David, an Episcopalian, this rising motif, as if a broad spiral stairway or an upward-climbing roadway encircling a mountain, suggested something theological. He noted the Methodist heritage of Emory and the exhortation of John Wesley, the founder of Methodism, for believers to "go on to perfection." In a way, this interior structure of the chapel implied an ascent of the faithful, step by step, toward a higher spiritual plane. Even in secular terms, one might think of the design as encouraging aspiration—the determination of a university, say, toward a higher degree of excellence.

The most poignant moment of the "long and dangerous journey" came along the banks of Nettie's Creek, at the bottom of the ravine in Baker Woodlands. Just a few feet from where Kilgo Circle meets the Mizell Bridge behind the Michael C. Carlos Museum, a narrow set of concrete steps descends into the ravine. The steps are the anchor of one arm of an environmental sculpture created by artist George Trakas in 1979 to commemorate the fiftieth anniversary of the Emory chapter of Phi Beta Kappa.

Source Route, as the sculpture is called, is the only artwork remaining of several environmental sculptures built on or near the Quadrangle for a weeklong symposium titled "Intellect and Imagination" in the fall of 1979. (The proceedings of this symposium were published the next spring in a special issue of *Daedalus* by the American Academy of Arts and Sciences, and the symposium heralded Emory's intention to join the national company of major research universities.) From a spot near the northern end of Mizell Bridge, half a dozen concrete steps, each about a foot wide, lead to a long steel plank sloping down toward the creek. At the end of the plank, six steel stairs extend down across an empty space where the bank has eroded over the decades. At the other end of the bridge, on the southern side of the stream, wooden steps lead down to eight-inch-wide wooden boards laid end to end and nailed into place on supporting struts to guide walkers to the stream bank opposite the metal staircase. The whole effect is of a large V whose imagined point lies in the streambed, and whose material arms reach up to grasp the ends of the bridge like a pincer.

Standing at the top of the concrete steps, David instructed his charges: go single file and in silence; say nothing; give the person in front of you four or five feet head start before you follow; pay attention to what you are feeling as you go down toward the stream; remain quiet when you reach the bottom.

One by one the students set off. At the juncture where the last concrete step meets the steel plank, some hesitancy stirred, some sense of vulnerability or uncertainty as a foot left the solid traction of the rough horizontal concrete and stepped onto the smooth and slanted steel. Then, with a little more sureness of balance, not quite on tiptoe but not heel first, each walker stepped down to the first metal stair. A bit of vertigo flickered at that first stair, which hung several feet above the sandy embankment. Then the knee released and bent for the next step down. Carefully the other foot moved forward, down, and stepped.

At last, everyone at the bottom, the group gathered half on one bank and half on the other, with David standing on a rock in the middle of the stream. The rippling of the water over stones and the depth of the ravine gave a sense of quiet isolation from the bustle of the campus some thirty feet above us. We had left the modern university and come, Thoreau-like, into the woods, not to dwell for long but for long enough.

"Where are we?" David asked.

"Beside a stream."

"Baker Woodlands."

"The end of a path."

"In a ravine."

"Ah," he said. "A ravine. Or we could say a valley, no? And if we said a valley, what valley might we be in?"

No response. A quiet pause.

"We are," David answered his own question, "in the valley that all of us must come to someday. We are in the place where the Psalmist laments and where the poet mourns. We are in the valley of the shadow of death."

David, himself wrenched by unthinkable tragedy several times in his life, offered a simple meditation on the occasional need for solitude, for silence, for tranquil consideration of the way failure, anguish, bewilderment, and death take us into the wilderness or down to the tangled depths—not an uncommon experience on a university campus.

Then he asked where he himself was standing.

"In the stream," said someone.

"At the point of a V," said another.

"Ah," said the phenomenologist; "what if you extended the arms of the V all the way from the ends of the bridge through the point where I'm standing and on down the hill—what would that make?"

"An X."

"Exactly! And what does X mark?"

"It marks the spot where the treasure is buried."

"Just so. Here in the place of your dark despair, if you have the courage to stay and dig long enough, you will find your treasure. Do not be afraid to linger here and find it."

Source Route, in Baker Woodlands.

CHAPTER 14

The Health Sciences and Clinical Care

WHILE THIS BOOK accentuates Emory as a place in the small town of Oxford and the area of metro Atlanta called Druid Hills, for many people the place known as Emory is found miles from either of those campuses. Emory as a place is, to them, Emory Healthcare facilities in midtown Atlanta, or far-flung clinics throughout the state of Georgia. In these places, perhaps more than on the two main campuses, the question of continuing institutional identity seems particularly acute. The MRI and CT scanners, the surgical suites and procedures, the infusion centers and specialty clinics bear little resemblance to the facilities of the hospital and school that became part of Emory in 1915. In just the past three decades, the scope of Emory Healthcare has grown to mammoth proportions, while the university's schools of medicine, nursing, and public health draw students, fellows, and faculty from around the globe and send graduates and researchers back into the wide world. In this range of complexity and extent, the health sciences at Emory differ little from their peer institutions around the country.

So the question raised in the introduction to this book arises again: in what sense, after all the parts have been replaced, is this the same car purchased so many decades ago? How is Emory Healthcare related to Wesley Memorial Hospital of 1905 and the early schools of medicine, nursing, and dentistry that became part of the university? And how does the experience of these spaces compare to the experience of other spaces in other eras?

Generations of portraits hang on the walls of hospital and clinic lobbies, and literally thousands of physicians, nurses, and staff members working throughout Emory Healthcare earned degrees at Emory thirty, forty, or more years ago. The stories and ethos of

the place are therefore present in pictures and persons. More than this, though, Emory as a place, a destination, a haven in which to stay for a time has constituted an arena of healing for more than a century. That legacy resides in the institution's bones, so to speak. For a place, the bones are its geography and structures.

In 1854, less than a decade after leaders of the small town of Terminus changed its name to Marthasville and then again to Atlanta, a group of physicians banded together to start a medical school. The Atlanta Medical College opened in city hall the next year, then moved in 1856 to new quarters on the site of the current Grady Memorial Hospital. Fifty years later, in 1906, following several splits and mergers, the Atlanta Medical College moved into a new building at the corner of Armstrong and Butler Streets, now the corner of Armstrong and Jesse Hill Jr. Drive, across from Grady Hospital.

In the wake of the 1910 publication of the Flexner Report—the landmark study of American medical schools by Abraham Flexner—leaders of the Atlanta Medical College recognized the value of affiliating with a university to enhance the scientific training and professional development of their students. Serendipitously, such a university came along in 1915, and the Atlanta Medical College petitioned the trustees of the new Emory University to merge. Thus was born, near Grady Memorial Hospital, the Emory University School of Medicine.

The 1906 Atlanta Medical College building, later Emory University School of Medicine. In 1961 the 1906 facility was razed to make way for an office building for faculty in the School of Medicine.

The Calico House, first home of Wesley Memorial (now Emory University) Hospital.

At the turn of the twentieth century, Atlanta had grown from its pre–Civil War size of about nine thousand residents to approximately ninety thousand, 40 percent of whom were African Americans. Only a handful of hospitals existed to care for this growing population. One of these was Grady Memorial, which the city had established in 1892 to care especially for the city's indigent population, both black and white. The North Georgia Conference of the Methodist Episcopal Church, South, aimed to fill the health-care gap by opening a new hospital. Stymied in their fund-raising, they appealed to Asa Griggs Candler Sr., who was not only among the wealthiest men in the city but also a devout Methodist. With his aid, in 1905 the Methodists opened Wesley Memorial Hospital in a building known as the Calico House, supposedly because its multi-colored wallpaper resembled calico cloth. The old house, which had served General William T. Sherman as his headquarters after the Battle of Atlanta in 1864, stood at the corner of Auburn Avenue and Courtland Street. Although it was not associated with the Atlanta Medical College, this hospital would merge with Emory University in 1915, the same year as the medical college. The hospital moved to new quarters on Clifton Road, at the Druid Hills campus, in

1922. Ambulances owned by Atlanta's funeral homes ferried the twenty-five patients to the new hospital facility.

Emory University Hospital was not the only part of the university born in the Calico House. The nursing program at Emory—now the Nell Hodgson Woodruff School of Nursing—also got its start at Wesley Memorial Hospital. Nurses in training lived in a boarding house next door to the Calico House. The nurses training program moved with the hospital to Druid Hills in 1922, and the program became a degree-granting school of the university in 1944.

With the establishment of the new Druid Hills campus in 1916, the university decided to move instruction in the basic sciences for the School of Medicine out to Druid Hills. Built in 1917, the original Hornbostel buildings for the School of Medicine bear the names of the two men who gave the funds to build them— the John P. Scott Laboratory of Anatomy and the T. T. Fishburne Laboratory of Physiology. Fishburne, from Virginia, had served as an Emory trustee and later bequeathed the funds to build the C. L. Fishburne Building in honor of his wife. Scott, too, was a trustee. The anatomy and physiology buildings had spiral staircases, which no longer met building codes when the laboratories underwent renovation in 1971–1973. Professor Elizabeth Lyon, of the Art History Department, played an instrumental part in saving the staircases from destruction by obtaining a waiver from the state. Although she sought to have these buildings included in the Emory District listed on the National Register of Historic Places, the registry deemed them too distant from the Quadrangle to be included.[1]

By the early 1970s, half a century after their construction, the anatomy and physiology buildings had ceased to be adequate for the much larger student body and the exponentially larger and more productive faculty in the School of Medicine. As the university prepared to renovate those first medical school labs, planners

The nurse in this photo at Wesley Memorial Hospital is identified as "Miss Newman," while the patient is identified as "Will Read, patient with osteomyelitis."

The John P. Scott Laboratory of Anatomy in 1917.

The T. T. Fishburne Physiology Building, built in 1917, stands to the right, with Trailertown in the background (see page 158). The one hundred trailers housed married students during the huge and rapid growth in enrollment after World War II.

seized the opportunity to enlarge the school's teaching space by connecting the two buildings. "The Connector," as it was called with little imagination, brought the campus its first, incongruous, Brutalist-style building. Not at all resembling the Hornbostel design of its wings, the blockish, fabricated concrete with its unadorned facade stood out like a pile of rubble in St. Peter's Square. In 2005, the university tore down this connector to make way for the James B. Williams Medical Education Building, dedicated in 2007 and designed to Hornbostel-like specifications, including marble cladding. Once again, the university renovated the anatomy and physiology buildings, this time adding the names of Charles and Peggy Evans to both buildings in memory of an appreciative patient and his wife.

When Robert W. Woodruff joined the Emory board of trustees in 1935, he began a habit of philanthropy primarily for the medical school and clinical services. By the early 1950s, even though he stepped down as a trustee in 1948, Woodruff was underwriting the annual deficit of the School of Medicine to the tune of a quarter million dollars.[2] Persuaded of a way to keep the school solvent and relieve him of covering these deficits perennially, Woodruff agreed to a plan drafted by Emory vice president Boisfeuillet Jones 1934C 1937L and presented by President Goodrich White 1908C. The proposal called for establishing a private clinic across Clifton Road

The Emory Clinic North Wing with the South Wing under construction, 1956.

from Emory University Hospital. Clinic physicians would devote a quarter of their time to teaching and would cover their own salaries as well as pay rent to the university to help meet the budget of the medical school.

Signed into being in January 1953, the Emory Clinic opened three years later with Dr. Hugh Wood as part-time director and seventeen faculty physicians. Dr. Elliott Scarborough succeeded Wood and served many years as the first full-time director. Scarborough had directed the cancer clinic that Woodruff helped Emory create with his first gift to the university in 1937. (That clinic is now the Winship Cancer Institute, named for Woodruff's maternal grandfather, Robert Winship, who had died of cancer.) When the new Emory Clinic opened in 1956, its north wing cost $1 million, paid for by Woodruff. Legend has it that the first time Woodruff saw the building, he remarked that it looked lopsided. Dr. Scarborough assured him that all would appear symmetrical after Mr. Woodruff paid for the south wing, placing the entrance in the middle. Woodruff wrote a check that day and said, "Here, Elliott. Build your damn building."[3]

The first building on campus dedicated solely to research was another gift from Robert W. Woodruff, this one to memorialize his father, Ernest Woodruff, who died in 1944. Funds, in fact, came from the Emily and Ernest Woodruff Foundation, which Robert and his brother George created from the estate of their parents and later renamed the Emily and Ernest Woodruff Fund. (In 1979, in what was then the largest gift to any educational institution in American history, the Woodruff brothers conveyed to Emory the entire corpus of this fund, valued then at $105 million—all in Coca-Cola stock.)

The Woodruff Memorial Building opened in 1952, just as Emory was embarking on a significant phase of growth. Only four years earlier, in 1948, Emory had awarded its first PhD degree, and the intention to build strong programs in research leading to the PhD demanded facilities that Emory had never before needed for undergraduate and professional programs. The top two floors of this eight-story building and the five-story south wing were not filled in until 1958, but by 1964 research activity had grown so much that two more stories had to be added to the south wing. In 1965, a seven-story north wing completed the structure, marking the rapid expansion of research in the health sciences.

While the Emory nursing school began life at the old Wesley Memorial Hospital in downtown Atlanta, the school took up quarters in the new hospital on Clifton Road after it opened in 1923,

The Woodruff Memorial Building.

A bas relief in the lobby of the
Woodruff Memorial Building.

Among the notables in this photo of the board of trustees, taken on November 8, 1946,
President Goodrich White stands at the far left. In front of him sits Robert W. Woodruff. Seated
second from the right is Lettie Pate Whitehead Evans, who in 1944 became the first woman
elected to the Emory board. Her first husband, Joseph B. Whitehead, had made a fortune bottling
Coca-Cola. After Whitehead's death in 1906, at the age of forty-two, Lettie continued to run the
business and eventually earned election to the Coca-Cola board of directors as one of the first
women in the country to serve on a corporate board of such magnitude. Later remarrying, she
gave generously to Agnes Scott College and other nonprofit enterprises as well as to Emory. The
location of this photo appears to be the amphitheater outside the Church School Building.

On the same day the trustees posed for their 1946 photo, the university dedicated the Joseph B. Whitehead Room in the Whitehead Pavilion of Emory University Hospital. The Whitehead Room owes its ornate plasterwork and carved wood to the design of architect Philip Trammell Shutze, who also designed Harris Hall and the Little Chapel in the Church School Building. He received an honorary doctorate from Emory in 1979.

On September 21, 1956, Emory signed an agreement with Egleston Children's Hospital—now part of Children's Healthcare of Atlanta—to provide medical services and a land lease for the hospital's new home on Clifton Road, next to the Emory Clinic. Seated at the table are Charles Howard Candler Sr., chair of the Emory board, and John A. Sibley, prominent Atlanta attorney and chair of the Egleston board. President Goodrich White, wearing a striped tie, stands behind Candler. Flora Glenn Candler, wife of the board chair and a patron of the arts, is the woman wearing the white hat. Through the next six decades, Egleston Hospital would be a vital partner with the Department of Pediatrics in the Emory School of Medicine.

then operated for a time out of Harris Hall (see page 157) and the old home of Arthur Tufts (see page 130). As the school outgrew its training facilities in the hospital, the dean and faculty searched for additional space to carry on their teaching. For many years the nursing school made a home for some of its work in one of the wooden barracks that served the university as classroom annexes. These "temporary" structures went up in 1946 to meet the expanded need for teaching space after World War II, but the last of the annexes did not come down until 2000, to make way for the Schwartz Center for Performing Arts.

After moving here and there, the nursing school at last got a "permanent" home with the dedication of a new building in 1970. Nell Hodgson Woodruff, a nurse who gave up her career to marry Robert W. Woodruff, maintained a lifelong devotion to nursing education and volunteer service. (During World War I, she helped train Red Cross nurses.) She attended the January 1968 groundbreaking ceremony for the school that afterward would bear her name, but she died before she could see the school open in its new space. The Woodruff School of Nursing moved again in 2001, out of its fortresslike Brutalist-style building to its current home at the corner of Clifton Road and Michael Street.

Like the School of Medicine and the School of Nursing, the Emory University School of Dentistry had its birth before the university was chartered in 1915. Established in 1887, the Atlanta-Southern Dental College was for many years the only dental school in Georgia, Florida, Alabama, and the Carolinas. In 1926 the school

The post–World War II home of the School of Nursing.

Nursing students, possibly in the 1950s, stroll down the steps in front of Emory University Hospital. The Physiology Laboratory peeks from behind the trees in the back.

New home for the School of Nursing under construction in 1969–1970.

moved into a new building at the corner of what is now Ralph McGill Boulevard and Courtland Street in downtown Atlanta. Eighteen years later, in 1944, the school merged with Emory to become the Emory University School of Dentistry.

The university sold that property in 1968 and, the following year, opened a modern facility at the corner of Clifton Road and Dantzler Drive (now Michael Street). As newer, state-supported dental schools in neighboring states increased competition during the following decades, the Emory University School of Dentistry shifted its focus to postgraduate specialty training and research. Despite significant research funding, financial pressures soon forced the closing of the school, and the last class of graduate fellows received their diplomas in 1992. For years afterward, the building continued to be called the Old Dental School Building, although it came to house the Health Sciences Library, some laboratories, and faculty offices. The university now refers to it simply by its street address, 1370–1462 Clifton.

As the health sciences at Emory grew in complexity and scope, the university administration and board of trustees brought them together under the umbrella of a central "health services" operation. In time, the administration of this vast web of clinical, educational, and research activities would need its own headquarters, and in 1977 the Robert W. Woodruff Health Sciences Center Administration

Home of the Atlanta-Southern Dental College, later Emory University School of Dentistry.

The newer home of the dental school, built on Clifton Road in 1969.

The Robert W. Woodruff Health Sciences Center Administration Building under construction.

Building (WHSCAB) met that need. Built in the Brutalist style popular at the time (used also for White Hall and the original Sanford S. Atwood Chemistry Center), the huge concrete building resembles the prow of a ship cutting boldly through the turbulent waves of healthcare reform into the future.

As late as the 1930s, malaria had a devastating impact on the South, a region dependent on agriculture and a workforce necessarily exposed to mosquitoes. In Baker County, Georgia, Robert W. Woodruff saw the effect of the disease on the men and women who lived around his Ichauway Plantation. With the help of Emory administrators and physicians, he established a field station and research center at his plantation in 1939. The station not only studied the malaria-carrying mosquitoes in the area but also provided treatment for affected citizens of the county.

Emory collaborated with Robert W. Woodruff to establish a field station on his Ichauway Plantation.

A visiting nurse makes a call on a family near Ichauway Plantation, circa 1940s.

Here the staff of the field station track data from test sites.

Field research included monitoring mosquito populations in the
marshy areas of Baker County.

During World War II, as U.S. military personnel were deployed to North Africa and the South Pacific—regions where malaria posed a significant threat to military effectiveness—the federal government established, in Atlanta, the Office of Malaria Control in War Areas to intensify the kind of work going on at Ichauway. After the war, this office would become the Communicable Disease Center— now the U.S. Centers for Disease Control and Prevention, which moved next door to the Emory campus with the help of Robert W. Woodruff. In time, collaborations between the Emory School of Medicine and the CDC would lead to the founding of one of the top schools of public health in the United States, the Rollins School of Public Health, named for one of the great families of Emory philanthropists, whose patriarch was trustee O. Wayne Rollins.

CHAPTER 15

Vanished Emory

ARCHAEOLOGISTS OF THE FUTURE will not spend any time digging up earth to find earlier layers of Emory University. Those earlier layers have been, for the most part, razed, carried off, and recycled or used for land fill elsewhere. They constitute an Emory that has vanished, except for traces left in the archives and in the memories of older alumni.

One exception to the truly vanished parts of Emory is a building that still stands about 225 miles from the Druid Hills campus and twenty minutes from the Florida border. The town of Valdosta, Georgia, in 1927 offered Emory forty-three acres to establish a junior college. It's not entirely clear why the citizens of the town did this. The state had established a "normal college," or teachers college, in Valdosta in 1906 but provided no funds to open it until 1913. Then, in 1922, the college was renamed Georgia State Woman's College, so perhaps the city's leaders were looking for gender balance from Emory, which at that time educated mostly (but not solely) men. Whatever the reason, the request came at an opportune time. Emory College was revamping its curriculum into a lower division and an upper division, requiring undergraduates to spend their first two years in a general-education course and their last two years in a specialized major. The new curriculum would easily accommodate a two-year program at a satellite campus.

Thus, in 1928, the university opened Emory-at-Valdosta. In addition to the acreage, the city provided a main building and a $200,000 endowment. With the beginning of a two-year program on the Oxford campus in 1929, undergraduates on the Valdosta, Oxford, and Atlanta campuses followed an identical curriculum. After completing two years on any of the three campuses, Emory

undergraduates had equal ground for success in their last two years of Emory College, the business school, or the nursing school.

Closed during World War II, Emory-at-Valdosta reopened after the war and reached a peak enrollment of nearly 250. But in 1950 the University System of Georgia made the women's college coeducational and renamed it Valdosta State College. Emory's recruitment base shrank in the face of lower state tuition for young men in south Georgia, and enrollment in the junior college sank to 65 in the spring of 1953. That May, facing the prospect of continuing deficits, the Emory trustees voted to offer the campus and its endowment to the University System of Georgia, which incorporated the land and buildings into Valdosta State.

Other parts of Emory have left little trace but still have a story worth remembering. One of these is the long-lost C. L. Fishburne Building on Clifton Road. Built in 1923, this structure stood for more than seven decades approximately where the Patterson Green now slopes down toward the Jenkins Courtyard behind the Goizueta Business School buildings. From the beginning of

The building shown here was the administration and classroom building of Emory-at-Valdosta. Now called Pound Hall, it houses the Harley Langdale Jr. College of Business Administration of Valdosta State University.

The C. L. Fishburne Building, now vanished from the site where the Goizueta Business School stands.

Emory's existence in Atlanta, the trustees had planned to establish a teachers college, which Chancellor Warren Candler told the board in 1916 was "scarcely less important than the School of Theology." The first professor of education, Ralph E. Wager, joined the faculty in 1921, and the C. L. Fishburne Building was intended as the first structure for the teachers college. Fernbank Elementary School, now part of the DeKalb County School System, had its birth here, and for decades the building housed the Department of Education (later the Educational Studies Division of the graduate school).

The Fishburne name honors the wife of Tipton Tinsley Fishburne, a member of the Methodist educational commission that chose Atlanta for the church's new university. Fishburne served as a trustee of Emory until his death in 1921. The Physiology Building bears his name in recognition of his contribution of $25,000 toward its construction. A memorial tribute by the board of trustees noted that his bequest of an additional $29,000 brought his total gifts to the university to $100,000—quite a sum in those days. Fishburne directed in his will that this last gift should go toward erecting a building that would bear the name of his wife, California "Callie" Lucretia Fishburne. It appears that Thomas H. English got the initials reversed in his 1965 history of Emory, calling it the L. C. Fishburne Building, an error repeated in many publications since.

As the business school grew in size and ambition, aiming to begin a PhD program and expand its MBA offerings, leaders of the school and the university focused on this prime corner as the new home for the school. Christened the Goizueta Business School when it opened in 1997, in memory of the late Emory trustee and CEO of the Coca-Cola Company Roberto C. Goizueta, the business school would expand eight years later into a second building, the Goizueta Foundation Center for Research and Doctoral Education. Meanwhile, the Division of Educational Studies moved to the North Decatur Building until the university began to phase out the division in 2012. Its last graduate students received their PhD degrees in 2017.

I have thought from time to time that it would be a worthwhile and beguiling remembrance of the past for the university to install a plaque in the sidewalk in front of the Goizueta Business School, like one of the stars on the Hollywood Walk of Fame. Here, though, the plaque would not bow to celebrity or stardom but would remind passersby of the generations of students who had learned how to be better teachers. The plaque could bear an image of the Fishburne Building engraved on brass and a few words of nostalgia about the building that once stood nearby, and what happened to it.

Other plaques in other squares of sidewalk around the campus could add up to a walk of history. Here, between Glenn Memorial and the Church School Building, a plaque embedded in the sidewalk could point to the place where Vice President Alben W. Barkley stood to deliver the Commencement address for his alma mater a half century after he had left its portals. Here, on the sidewalk beside the Depot, another marker might indicate where ROTC students greeted Marshal Foch in 1921. Another one here could denote the presence, decades ago, of Trailertown and its young married couples after World War II. Another one here could mark the site of Jimmy Carter's speech for the groundbreaking of Cannon Chapel.

The illustrations in this chapter offer a few more contenders for the "walk of history" to commemorate a vanished Emory.

To house the growing number of married students, in 1959 Emory constructed the Clifton Court Apartments—one hundred units ranging from efficiencies to three-bedroom apartments. The entire project cost just over $1 million. At the time, married students were living in decade-old "substandard apartments" in an area dubbed Mudville, near the current CDC campus. Some 320 of the 830 married students at Emory lived in university-owned housing. These Clifton Court Apartments would be renovated in the late 1980s to create Turner Village, a residential hub for theology students that was dedicated in September 1990. In addition to renovating the apartments, the theology school built a conference center (shown here) and a small chapel in the area. Turner Village and the conference center were demolished to make way for the Emory Conference Center Hotel, which opened in 1995.

Robert Cotter Mizell 1911C served Emory for more than forty years as director of development and trustee, among other responsibilities. A confidant of Robert W. Woodruff, Mizell encouraged the Coca-Cola magnate to become a major benefactor of Emory. This stairway, erected in Mizell's memory after his death in 1955, stood near the end of the bridge that now bears his name (see page 162). In 1993, pressed for space to accommodate the growing collections of the Michael C. Carlos Museum, the university demolished the stairway and filled in this gap on the southern side of the Quadrangle with the new Michael Graves–designed museum building. The original Hornbostel plan for the Quad had suggested a building in this space, so the construction of the museum in a way completed a design nearly eighty years old. The memorial plaque on the stairway was preserved and added to the east wall of the museum building beside a smaller set of stairs that lead under a pergola from the Quad to Kilgo Circle.

Ruel B. Gilbert Hall and William D. Thomson Hall, both constructed in 1947, helped meet the huge need for housing in the post–World War II enrollment explosion. Gilbert was a Methodist layman who had designated his bequest for construction of a dormitory for theology students. Thomson, Emory College class of 1895, was an Atlanta attorney who served as a trustee of Emory, twice served as acting dean of the law school, and was for many years general counsel of the university. (His home, which he sold to Emory in 1943, stood at the present site of Gambrell Hall, on the corner of Clifton and North Decatur Roads. It served as the university president's home until President Sanford Atwood moved into Lullwater in 1963.)

The house in the distance in this photo stands on Oxford Road, and the hillside in the left of the photo is the site of the Atwood Chemistry Center. Known as Gil-Thom, Gilbert and Thomson Halls were razed in 2007 to make way for reorienting Eagle Row (formerly Fraternity Row) and creating space for the new Psychology and Interdisciplinary Studies Building (PAIS). History-conscious architects saved the wrought-iron arched grills above the Gil-Thom doorways to enhance a small garden between PAIS and the Atwood Chemistry Center.

These elegant apartment buildings for married students lined Uppergate Drive at about where the Winship Cancer Institute now stands. Completed in 1951, they remained in use for some twenty years before giving way to a student clinic, which in turn was razed to make way for the Winship Cancer Institute in 2003.

This water tower stood above the campus like a sentry, as if to guard against drought and keep watch for welcome rain clouds on the horizon. It should have been painted white, with trompe l'oeil stippling to mimic the look of a golf ball. After someone referred to it as "the Bobby Jones Memorial," no one ever again could see it as anything but a golf ball on a tee. (In 1930, Atlanta native Bobby Jones 1929L became the only person ever to win the grand slam of golf. The Bobby Jones Scholarship sends Emory graduates to the University of St. Andrews every year and welcomes St. Andrews grads to Emory.) The tower was installed in 1933. By 2007, it had become, in a term that Bobby Jones would have appreciated, a hazard. The tower had not held water since the 1980s, and improvements to maintain its structural integrity were estimated to cost several hundred thousand dollars. While realigning Eagle Row to make way for new residence halls, the university dismantled the tower and recycled its steel.

Scrambling to create additional teaching space as enrollment doubled following World War II, the university in 1947 built three temporary classroom buildings, or annexes, as they were called. Annexes B and C (above) stood between the C. L. Fishburne Building and the later site of the Schwartz Center for Performing Arts. Through the years, these old barracks housed various programs—Annex A: the Air Force ROTC program, Upward Bound, and the Reading Clinic; Annex B: nursing and art history; and Annex C: fine arts, theater studies, music rehearsal rooms, and much later, administrative offices. During the 1950s Annex C housed chemistry labs, which Professor Leon Mandell, chair of the Chemistry Department, described in 1959 as "not just inadequate but literally . . . a danger to life. The plumbing leaks badly (to the extent that we have had to drill holes in the floor for the water to run off so as to be able to work); there are gas leaks; the electrical system has been condemned by an inspector; the roof leaks water into our stockroom" (Emory University, Office of Business Management Collection). Annex A was demolished in April 1974 to make way for the Woodruff Health Sciences Center Administration Building (page 187). The last annex to go was Annex C, razed in 2000 after fifty-three years of "temporary" service, to make way for the Schwartz Center, whose loading dock stands about where Annex C once stood.

Students and faculty members could drop off their mail and pick up their prescriptions with one stop at the corner of Clifton Road and Haygood Drive. This building housed Ivey's Drug Store, to the left, and the U.S. Post Office for "EMORY UNIV, GA," to the right. The Center for Rehabilitation Medicine would fill this corner in the 1970s, across the street from the Woodruff Health Sciences Administration Building.

Emory officially opened the door for residential coeducation in 1953, although women had received degrees from all schools of the university by then—including more than two hundred graduates of Emory College. The residential presence of women, however, led quickly to the organizing of sororities to match the vibrant fraternity life. Ten sororities received charters at Emory in 1959, and a decade later sorority lodges were constructed at the corner of Clifton and what is now Gambrell Drive, across from the MacMillan Law Library. Replaced by new lodges on Eagle Row (formerly Fraternity Row) near the Campus Services complex, the old lodges were razed in 2004 to make way eventually for the J Wing of Emory University Hospital.

When the Candler School of Theology moved into the Old Theology Building on the Quadrangle, in 1916, the school had ample room for classes, offices, a library, and even a chapel. Within four decades, however, postwar enrollment, a growing library, and a greatly expanded faculty to teach the quadrupled student body meant the school needed new space. Bishops Hall was the answer. With funds raised mostly by the Methodist bishops of the Southeast, the school broke ground in January 1957 and dedicated the building in September that year. For another half-century, Bishops Hall served generations of theologians and ministers, while the parking around it was whittled to nothing and new buildings cropped up nearby. By 2008, when the Candler School opened the new Rita Anne Rollins Building, Bishops Hall was doomed. The dismantling of the well-used structure in 2013 made way for the new Pitts Theology Library building. This photo was taken from where Rudolph Courtyard would take shape in 1979–1980.

When the Emory trustees named this 1940 residence hall for Bishop Holland
Nimmons McTyeire, they may have wanted to commemorate the ties of the
Methodist Episcopal Church, South, to Vanderbilt University. McTyeire, a leading
Southern Methodist bishop, had helped to found Vanderbilt in 1873 by acquiring the
million-dollar gift from Commodore Cornelius Vanderbilt, whose second wife was a
cousin of the bishop's wife. The Emory trustees also may have wanted to comment on
the reunification of the southern and northern branches of Methodism the previous
year. Bishop McTyeire and Commodore Vanderbilt saw their university as a means
of forging new unity in the nation shortly after the Civil War. (McTyeire himself had
been a defender of slavery before the war.) The demolition of McTyeire Hall in 2015
made way for the construction of the new Campus Life Center.

This 1917 photo, with its rustic bridge and wooded path, underscores
the semirural setting of the early Atlanta campus. The lay of the land
suggests that the bridge may have been located where a grove of trees now
separates Oxford Road from the Math and Science Center.

CHAPTER 16

The View from 407

TO GIVE A SENSE OF HOW "Emory as place" has changed—become busier in its Brownian motion of scurrying people, grown more complex in its worldwide reach and local affiliations—I offer as evidence suite 407 in the Administration Building. For decades, this small set of rooms housed the Office of the University Secretary, until that office moved into new digs in the Old Theology Building (see page 89).

It's an odd job, the role of university secretary. For one thing, it's nothing that anyone grows up aspiring to be—or even knows about. No child says, "I want to be a university secretary one day." Besides, the workload sounds impossibly overwhelming: secretary to the whole university? How many people can one person take dictation from? It's true that the title occasionally leads to amusing mistakes. Once when I was the university secretary, a piece of presorted mail with a label on it arrived. The character limitation of the label cut off part of my title, and I found myself addressed as "Secretary of the Univers." Now that would be a fascinating job.

President Harvey Cox announced the creation of the position of university secretary in his annual report to the trustees in 1925. The chief purpose of the job back then seems to have been to support the university's first major capital campaign, launched in 1926 with the aim of raising $10 million in ten years. E. C. Lovett was first to fill the role, which mostly entailed what we now call development, or fund-raising. Sadly, the crash of Wall Street in 1929 and the onset of the Great Depression put a premature end to the "Ten Million in Ten Years" campaign. The crash also may have put a premature end to Lovett's career as university secretary, since Emory history records nothing further about him.[1]

From the fall of 1991 to the spring of 2005, suite 407 served as my second home—the post from which to organize Commencement and convocations and inaugurations; the bunker in which to hunker while drafting presidential speeches and annual reports and citations for honorary degrees and other recognitions; the transom over which passed every sort of request from across the campus and beyond; and, not incidentally, the hub of trustee planning, logistics, activities, and records. For this office was accountable for making sure that minutes of trustee meetings were properly recorded and archived for posterity. With all that activity in suite 407, the place often felt (as a colleague once remarked about the Emory College dean's office) like a blender with its speed set on high. The occupants of 407 might have been forgiven for thinking their suite was the hub of a fast-turning wheel; in truth, the Quadrangle outside was that hub.

Happily, the window overlooking the Quad provided perspective. The lawn spreading out below my window presented daily reminders that life at Emory involved play as well as work, protest as well as study, startling distraction as well as earnest endeavor. From the fourth floor of the Administration Building, my perch invited occasional glances to the scene below, where I found small moments of delight or surprise.

One winter's day, while looking away from my computer screen toward the leaf-bare trees outside, I spied the president of the university, William M. Chace, striding away from the Administration Building, past Carlos Hall, toward the east and Candler Library. About midway there, he looked across the Quad and waved at someone. Following the direction of his gaze, I saw, on the other side of the Quad, his wife, JoAn Chace, walking in the opposite direction. They turned from their parallel but opposing paths onto the sidewalk at the middle of the Quad, met at the flagpole, and spoke for a moment, then they exchanged a quick kiss and continued in their respective directions away from each other. It was a salutary moment of affection in the middle of what was probably a busy day. It was also a reminder that the university is not just a place of world-changing research and mind-shaping instruction but also a habitat for men and women in the regular rounds of life.

Another time, I looked up from the computer to catch, for just a second and a half, the furious beating of wings outside my window as a red-tailed hawk flew up and past, toward the roof of the building, with a hapless squirrel in its talons. The pecan trees on the

The Quadrangle as it looked in 1928.

Quad offer the countless Emory squirrels an abundant harvest but also a dangerous gantlet under the gaze of circling predators.

Always, it seemed, students populated the Quad below on sunny days, throwing Frisbees, tossing footballs, playing catch with softballs, bathing in the sun, or sitting in circles around the teachers they had cajoled into meeting outside. Despite the expansion of the campus far beyond the historic Quad, the lawn stretching below me continued to have the feel of the heart of the place.[2]

The late John Stone, for nearly forty years a faculty member in the School of Medicine, until his death in 2008, also graced the university and the world with poetry. He published five books of poetry as well as two collections of essays. Founder of the emergency medicine residency program at Grady Memorial Hospital, he served for many years as dean of admissions for the medical school and taught one of the first courses in the nation on medicine in literature. In a poem titled "The Spirits of This Lawn," commissioned for the inauguration of President James W. Wagner in 2004, John evoked the "Genii Loci," the "timeless spirits" of the Quad:

> For let us consider the spirits of this lawn
>   who have gathered to speak with us
> For the daffodils have flared in fanfare
>   the bagpipes have skirled
>   the brass and bells have sounded.[3]

Yes—the brass and bells. John reminds me that not only do the bagpipes of Commencement sound in this almost-sacred space, but so do the bells and horns and chants of Tibetan monks, when the university celebrates Emory-Tibet Week every March. In front of the Michael C. Carlos Museum, strings of bright prayer flags of blue, red, yellow, and white stretch from tree to tree and flutter in the springtime breezes. Smoke arises from a clay, charcoal-burning stove during the Sangsol offerings prepared by Tibetan Buddhist monks. Cymbals clang, horns blare, temple bells sound. Prayers go forth in hope of auspicious days in the week ahead.

Here, too, each December 1—World AIDS Day—the lawn is spread with scores of large, colorful quilts that honor the memory of men and women who have died of AIDS. The Quilt on the Quad, an annual commemoration sponsored by Emory Hillel since 2005, constitutes the largest display on any college campus of panels from the Names Project AIDS Memorial Quilt. Cared for by the Names Project Foundation, headquartered in Atlanta, the AIDS quilt comprises some forty-nine thousand panels representing nearly a hundred thousand persons. Each panel, created by friends or family of a victim of AIDS, memorializes with images, words, and mementos the incalculable value of a human life. Between classes or on their way to meetings, Emory community members pause to stroll between the swaths of lovingly stitched cloth to peer at photos and read remembrances.

The Quad has served as a classroom, not only for students fortunate enough to enjoy seminars alfresco on pleasant afternoons but also for hundreds of faculty, students, and staff members gathered to talk about issues of great moment. Before the invasion of Iraq, in 2003, the Student Government Association organized a "Classroom on the Quad" and invited faculty members, veterans, staff members, and student leaders to offer differing perspectives on the wisdom or folly of war. In subsequent years, topics for the Classroom on the Quad ranged from immigration to the future of military service and the importance of civic duties like voting.

Here on the Quad, too, the Emory community has gathered after unimaginable tragedy. On the evening of September 12, 2001, the day after the terrorist destruction of the World Trade Center, the dean of the chapel organized a candlelight vigil for silent prayer and remembrance of those who had died in the catastrophe, including Emory alumni and family members of Emory students. On April 23, 2007, candles again lit the Quad as the community gathered to reflect in

Students gathered on the steps of Candler Library in May 1969 to demand greater resources for African American students and better pay for cafeteria workers.

the aftermath of the shooting at Virginia Tech that left thirty-three people dead. More than three decades earlier, on May 4, 1970, the university community spent the afternoon gathered on the Quad to remember students killed at Kent State University two days before and to hear members of both major political parties speak about the war in Vietnam. The afternoon concluded with a "love feast."

Wounds to the Emory community itself have prompted gatherings on this hallowed lawn. I watched from my window in the spring of 1992 as a silent procession moved slowly down the walkway on the far side of the Quad, past the Old Theology Building, toward the Administration Building and into it. Perhaps two hundred or more Emory students, faculty members, staff, and friends from beyond the campus climbed the stairs to the fourth floor to request a meeting with President James Laney. Their grievance: the perceived lack of action by the university following the harassment of two freshman males seen kissing in a public space. This harassment and intimidation violated the university's own policy prohibiting discriminatory harassment on the basis of sexual orientation. Now the community of LGBTQ persons at Emory and their many allies wanted Emory to reaffirm its commitment to protect them. No, more—they wanted the university to confirm its willingness to welcome them, support them, and recognize them as vital contributors to the place called Emory. The President's Office offered them Cokes, and the president met with them for an hour, after which the appointment of a task force and months of hard work led Emory to become the first private university in the South to make sexual orientation a protected category in its nondiscrimination policy.

The Quad has provided public space for other protests as well. The first may have occurred in the spring of 1968, when students gathered on the Quad to demand a fine arts center.[4] Both the manner and the focus of the demonstration differed significantly from what was happening elsewhere that spring. At Columbia University, for instance, students occupied buildings to protest the Vietnam War and to demand reconsideration of a gym that would create a barrier between the campus and nearby Harlem.

Concerns of racial justice would come to the Quad the following year, in the spring of 1969, when the Black Student Alliance (BSA) called attention to ways it believed the university was falling short in meeting the special challenges faced by black students in a predominantly white institution. Among the requests made public by the BSA in March 1969, one sought greater salary equity for food-service employees, a majority of whom were African American. On Sunday, May 25, black students frustrated by the slow response of the administration stood during the worship service in the chapel of the Old Theology Building. They lifted signs protesting what university chaplain Richard Devor afterward called "the racism of

Dental school alumni and students, on the Quad in 1986, protest the decision to close the dental school, which awarded its last DDS degrees two years later and its last postgraduate degrees in 1992.

the Christian Community of Emory." The students then led a silent procession out the building, through the Quad, to Cox Hall, where some of them stayed through much of the next four days in a picket line at the entrance to the cafeteria.

On Wednesday, May 28, more than five hundred students and faculty members gathered on the Quad to support the protesting students. In the end, President Sanford Atwood—after conversations with SGA president Charles Haynes 1971C 1985G and BSA president Henry "Hank" Ambrose 1969C—resolved the impasse by acknowledging that racism existed on campus.

Out of this contretemps came a number of initiatives, including the first black studies program at a private southern university, the appointment of the first African American administrator at Emory (Marvin Arrington Sr. 1967L), and the establishment of the President's Commission on the Status of Minorities (later renamed the President's Commission on Race and Ethnicity, and later still folded into the Advisory Committee on Community and Diversity).

More protests would follow through the years: in 1986, against the closing of the dental school; in 1992, in support of LGBTQ equity; in 2011, in support of higher pay and better benefits for contract workers in food services, parking, and transportation; in 2012, against cuts to programs and departments in Emory College and the Laney Graduate School; and in 2014, at nearby Rudolph Courtyard, in support of the Black Lives Matter movement.

Of protests against injustice there will never be an end, because, unfortunately, injustice will always be around to be protested. Yet the opportunity (the responsibility) remains for a university to ensure that the voices of the meek as well as the mighty can be heard. That really is the true work of the university—to provide a forum for the full cacophony of ideas, from the foolish to the wise, from the half-baked and inarticulate to the fully thought-out and eloquently stated. As the preamble to the original bylaws of the university puts it: "Emory University was founded . . . for the promotion of the broadest intellectual culture in harmony with the democratic institutions of our country and permeated by the principles and influences of the Christian religion. It is designed to be a profoundly religious institution without being narrowly sectarian. It proposes to encourage freedom of thought as liberal as the limitations of truth."

Such freedom and liberality flourish in a space like the Quad—in a place like Emory. That realization made the view from 407 worth daily thanks.

This photo of the Quad predates the Administration Building and shows in the shadowed distance a sundial that stood beside the central walkway until sometime in the 1940s. The lampposts and the concrete walkway down the middle likewise are gone—as is the solitary figure standing there taking in the view of the buildings and landscape. Professor or student, male or female, staff or visitor—whoever it was, maybe that person stood there long enough to shape a memory and in turn be shaped by the spirit of the place.

Acknowledgments

This book has gestated in some fashion for more than thirty years, beginning with a piece of writing I did for the Emory libraries in 1986. I was working then as the reference librarian in the Pitts Theology Library of the Candler School of Theology. Thomas H. English, professor emeritus of English and ninety-one years old, was compiling a booklet with chapters devoted to the history of each of the nine principal libraries at Emory. During his long career of teaching at Emory (from 1925 until his retirement in 1964), he had been a particular devotee of the library and friend to librarians, helping to identify resources, build collections, and publish articles and reprints of some of the manuscripts and rare books in what was then called Special Collections. He also had written the 1965 chronicle of Emory's first half century in Atlanta. My task of writing a history of the theology library introduced me to one of the more memorable characters from Emory history whom I have had the privilege of meeting personally.

The writing of the library's history overlapped with another bit of retrospective work. In 1987, the president's office—with the gracious consent of my boss, the director of the theology library, Channing Jeschke—hired me to spend half my work hours on a special project. The occasion was the conclusion of the first ten years of James Laney's presidency, and the required product was to be an accounting—modest but proud, full but simple—of what the university had accomplished during that time. The university had celebrated its sesquicentennial just a year before, so the finished work became a kind of binocular view—one eye looking at the previous decade, and the other eye looking back a century and a half. The booklet was titled "Emory at 150: A Report on the State of the University," and the experience of scouring the record to develop that narrative was my introduction to the larger history of Emory. For the next three decades, until the fall of 2016, I would serve as university secretary and then vice president and deputy to the president, writing annual reports and speeches and ceremonial language, editing communications, and—especially where this book is concerned—delving repeatedly into the minutes of the trustees and old annual reports of deans and vice presidents to find the answers to why things had turned out or been done the way they had.

The book in hand would not have been possible without the staff of the Stuart A. Rose Manuscript, Archives, and Rare Book Library. That extraordinary library boasts not only one of the great collections of literary and cultural archives in the Southeast but also the best collection of archivists, librarians, curators, subject specialists, and student employees one could hope for. My gratitude abounds to reference coordinator Kathy Shoemaker for her patience in answering my countless questions; to university archivist John Bence for his knowledge of the collections and insight into where to search for answers; to the head of research services Courtney Chartier and her team of staff and student assistants for their management of requests and gathering of materials; to archivists Sarah Quigly, Elizabeth Russey Roke, Rebecca Sherman, Laura Starratt, and Dorothy Waugh for their expertise; and to Christeene Alcosiba, Charmaine Bonner, Gabrielle Dudley, Carrie Hintz, Jennifer Meehan, Meaghan O'Riordan, Elizabeth Shoemaker, and Anita Vanucci for their willing help at every turn.

Thanks also to the staff of Pitts Theology Library, especially Richard "Bo" Manly Adams Jr., Brandon Wason, and Debra Madera.

Ann Borden Watson, senior director of Emory Photo/Video, and her colleague Kay Hinton were helpful in locating photos not found in the archives, especially those of the Hardman Cemetery and the Administration Building.

Sally Wolff King, with whom I collaborated in editing the volume *Where Courageous Inquiry Leads*, which contains many short essays about Emory history from several dozen authors, provided invaluable assistance for this book. I am grateful for her knowledge of the health sciences, her relentless fact checking, and her editorial suggestions.

I owe special thanks to the former director of Rose Library, Rosemary Magee, who several years ago suggested an affiliation with the library in my role as unofficial historian of Emory University—a role that became official in October 2015. My thanks to James W. Wagner, now president emeritus of Emory, for his agreement back then to make that appointment official, and to Emory's current president, Claire E. Sterk, for graciously continuing that arrangement.

John Patrick Allen, editor at the University of Georgia Press, found external reviewers of the manuscript who not only understood the aims of the book but also made observations in their reviews that gave me fresh insight into my own work. This was an unlooked for gift, and although they recommended publishing the book as it was, I took their observations as an impetus to improve on the original. I hope that those reviewers, whoever they were, will find the revisions worthy of their very keen reading. I am grateful as well to Thomas Roche, of the University of Georgia Press, for his guidance and advice as this project wound through the editorial and design process. I owe a debt as well to Courtney Denney for her superb copy editing.

First and last, I owe great thanks to Sara Haigh Hauk for her enduring encouragement, support, and optimism in all things that aim for the good. This book certainly is intended as such a thing, and any hit short of the mark is solely owing to my errant aim.

All photographs are from the Emory University Archives in the Stuart A. Rose Library of Emory University, with five exceptions. The photos of the Hardman Cemetery on page 83 and the exterior of the Administration Building on page 97 are from Emory Photo/Video. The two photos of Callanwolde on page 69 are printed courtesy of Callanwolde Fine Arts Center. The photo of the Asa Candler mansion (now St. John Chrysostom Melkite Catholic Church on Ponce de Leon Avenue, Atlanta) on page 68 is courtesy of Special Collections and Archives, Georgia State University Library.

Notes

INTRODUCTION. *Genius Loci*

1. Online Etymology Dictionary, s.v. "campus," accessed September 5, 2018, https://www.etymonline.com/word/campus.

2. Marshall P. Duke, "'Emory Are Here': Emory as Place and Story," in *Where Courageous Inquiry Leads: The Emerging Life of Emory University*, ed. Gary S. Hauk and Sally Wolff King (Atlanta, Ga.: Emory University, 2010), 3–12.

3. A note about class years: the class affiliation of Emory graduates is designated by following the graduate's name with the year of graduation and an abbreviation of the school that awarded the degree: B for business, C for Emory College, D for dentistry, G for graduate, L for law, Lib for librarianship, M for medicine, N for nursing, Ox for Oxford College, PH for public health, PhD for that degree, T for theology, V for Valdosta, and H for honorary.

4. Emory University, Office of the Provost, "Faculty Handbook," chap. 2, accessed May 2, 2018, http://provost.emory.edu/faculty/handbook/chapters/two.html.

CHAPTER 1. Oxford

1. Georgia Conference Manual Labor School minutes, July 17, 1835, Stuart A. Rose Manuscript, Archives, and Rare Book Library, Emory University.

2. Erik Blackburn Oliver, *Cornerstone and Grove: A Portrait in Architecture and Landscape of Emory's Birthplace in Oxford, Georgia* (Oxford, Ga.: Oxford College of Emory University, 2009), 21.

3. Henry Morton Bullock, *A History of Emory University* (Nashville, Tenn.: Parthenon Press, 1936), 115.

4. John D. Thomas, "Enigma: A Ring around Oxford," *Emory Magazine*, Spring 1998, http://www.emory.edu/EMORY_MAGAZINE/spring98/enigmabell.html.

5. Undated, unsigned manuscript, Emory University Archives series 47, box 1, folder 17, Emory College General Records, Stuart A. Rose Library.

6. M. B. Summerlin, letter to his father, October 18, 1851, series 6, box 4, Emory College General Records.

7. Oxford Historical Society, "George Washington Whitfield Stone Sr.," accessed May 7, 2018, http://www.oxfordhistoricalsociety.org /gww-stone-sr.html.

8. Emory College, *Catalogue of Emory College, Oxford, Georgia, 1904–1905*, 38, Stuart A. Rose Library.

9. "Dooley's Letter," *Emory Phoenix*, October 1909, 13, Stuart A. Rose Library.

10. Atticus Greene Haygood, report of the president to the Board of Trustees, minutes, June 23, 1883, Emory College Trustee Records, Stuart A. Rose Library.

11. Minutes, October 15, 1915, Emory College Trustee Records, Stuart A. Rose Library.

12. Scott Henry, "Razed in Atlanta: Six Great Buildings We Lost," *Atlanta Magazine*, February 14, 2017, http://www.atlantamagazine.com/ news-culture-articles/razed-atlanta-6-great-buildings-lost/.

13. Bullock, *A History of Emory University*, 221–23.

14. For the full story of athletics at Emory, see Clyde Partin Sr., *Athletics for All: A History of Health, Physical Education, Athletics, and Recreation at Emory University, 1836–2005*, ed. Gary S. Hauk (Atlanta, Ga.: Emory/Lenz, 2006).

15. Ibid., 237–38.

16. Correspondence, July 14, 1914, Asa Griggs Candler Papers, Stuart A. Rose Library; for the seventy-five acres, see minutes, March 31, 1915, Emory University, Board of Trustee Records, Stuart A. Rose Library.

17. For a full account of the vagaries of the Oxford campus since 1915, see Joseph C. Moon, *An Uncommon Place: Oxford College of Emory University*, rev. ed. (Oxford, Ga.: Oxford College of Emory University, 2003–2014).

CHAPTER 2. Emory's Early Entwinement with Slavery

1. Mark Auslander, *The Accidental Slaveowner: Revisiting a Myth of Race and Finding an American Family* (Athens: University of Georgia Press, 2011).

CHAPTER 3. Aerial Campus Views

1. Minutes, February 8, 1837, Emory College Trustee Records, Stuart A. Rose Library; on July 10, the trustees changed leases to sales but maintained the stipulations against gaming and spirits.

2. Oliver, *Cornerstone and Grove*, 14.

3. Emory Environs Collection, Emory University Archives series 104, box 1, folder 10.

CHAPTER 4. The Trees in the Forest

1. George G. Smith, *Life and Times of George Foster Pierce* (Sparta, Ga.: Hancock, 1888), 378–79, quoted in Bullock, *A History of Emory University*, 60.

2. F. M. Means, "History of Emory College," [circa 1880], in Alexander Means Papers, MSS 151, box 2, folder 9, Stuart A. Rose Library.

3. Nancy Seideman, "Lullwater and the Greening of Emory: Catalyst for a New Environmental Commitment," in *Where Courageous Inquiry Leads*, ed. Hauk and Wolff King, 71–81.

4. The phrase "Room to Breathe: The Candler Estate" appears on the cover of the November 1958 issue of *Emory Alumnus*.

5. William H. Murdy and Eloise Carter, "A Report on the Status of Forested Land of Emory University," July 1986, series 29, box 25, Emory University Senate Records, Stuart A. Rose Library.

6. Andrew B. Calhoun, grandfather of F. Phinizy Calhoun Sr., was a physician who helped found the Atlanta Medical College, which later became Emory University School of Medicine. Phinizy's father, Abner W. Calhoun, was an eminent ophthalmologist in his own right and for many years was the sole ear-and-eye specialist in the Southeast. The first library of the School of Medicine was named for him. Phinizy Sr. also had a son, Phinizy Jr., who burnished the family legacy in ophthalmology at Emory still more brightly.

7. Jimmy Powell (director of engineering and exterior services, Emory University), interview by author, May 18, 2017.

8. Jon Gunnemann, email message to author, January 12, 2018.

CHAPTER 5. Candler Homes

1. See Gary S. Hauk and Sally Wolff King, "The Charles Howard Candler Professors," in *Where Courageous Inquiry Leads*, ed. Hauk and Wolff King, 293–302.

2. For a thorough history of the Candler family, see Ann Uhry Abrams, *Formula for Fortune: How Asa Candler Discovered Coca-Cola and Turned It into the Wealth His Children Enjoyed* (Bloomington, Ind.: iUniverse, 2012).

CHAPTER 6. Naming the Streams

1. Richard H. Sams, "The Hardman Cemetery and Meeting House, the Shallowford Indian Trail, and the Houston Chapel" (unpublished paper), DeKalb, Georgia, History Center Archives.

2. Vivian Price, *The History of DeKalb County, Georgia, 1822–1900* (Fernandina Beach, Fla.: Wolfe, 1997), 390–91.

3. The Emory alma mater, written in 1918 by J. Marvin Rast 1918C 1929T and sung to the tune of "Annie Lisle" (probably the most-used tune in America for alma maters) begins, "In the heart of dear old Emory, where the sun doth shine, / That is where our hearts are turning, 'round old Emory's shrine."

CHAPTER 7. The Quadrangle

1. Vanderbilt University (website), "History of Vanderbilt University," accessed May 10, 2018, https://www.vanderbilt.edu/about/history/. For a full account of the split between Vanderbilt and the Methodist Episcopal Church, South, see Paul Keith Conklin, *Gone with the Ivy: A Biography of Vanderbilt University* (Knoxville: University of Tennessee Press, 1985), 149–84.

CHAPTER 8. Commencement

1. Thomas H. English, *Emory University, 1915–1965: A Semicentennial History* (Atlanta, Ga.: Emory University, 1965), 33.

CHAPTER 14. The Health Sciences and Clinical Care

1. Former Emory University archivist Ginger Cain, in an email to Charlie Andrews dated October 3, 2002, explains the reason why the National Registry rejected the 1973 application by Elizabeth Lyon to include the anatomy and physiology buildings in the Emory University District. The original application and related correspondence are in series 104, box 1, folder 10, the Emory Environs Collection, Emory University Archives.

2. Minutes, November 14, 1957, Emory University, Board of Trustees Records, Stuart A. Rose Library. That year the board failed to persuade Mr. Woodruff to begin serving again as a trustee. The minutes note his "feeling that he could be of greater service to the University if he were not a member of the board."

3. The anecdote about Woodruff's response to Scarborough comes from former Emory Clinic director and vice president for health affairs

Charles R. Hatcher and former Emory Clinic executive administrator Roy Townsend by way of Sally Wolff King, Woodruff Health Sciences Center historian and author of a forthcoming book on the history of the Emory Clinic. For the history of the birth of the clinic, see *Where Courageous Inquiry Leads*, ed. Hauk and Wolff King, 399–400 and 447–55.

CHAPTER 16. The View from 407

1. Mr. Lovett was succeeded by the eminent Robert Cotter Mizell 1911C, a man of many talents and later the first director of development of the university. During the presidencies of Goodrich White, Walter Martin, and Sanford Atwood, the title of university secretary was changed to assistant to the president and assistant secretary of the board, noting the twin responsibilities to board and president. Among those filling the role were Robert F. Whitaker 1926C 1927L, who later served in other positions until his death in 1969; Charles H. "Pete" McTier 1961B, who would leave for the Woodruff Foundation, which he later served as president; and John Stephenson 1970C, who would have a stint as vice president for development before becoming executive director of the J. Bulow Campbell Foundation. President Atwood, having been an Ivy League provost before coming to Emory, resurrected the more customary northeastern title of university secretary for Stephenson. J. Thomas Bertrand succeeded Stephenson in 1978 and hired me as assistant university secretary ten years later to do much of the writing required of the office. When he left in 1991, President Laney appointed me to the secretary's role, which I filled through the rest of his administration, Billy Frye's interim presidency, and Bill Chace's nine years as president, when I gained the additional title of vice president. When Jim Wagner began his presidency in 2003, I suggested that the job had grown too large for one person, as I was then a kind of chief of staff as well as university secretary. He agreed to carve off the secretary's work from my duties as deputy to the president, and in 2005 he recruited Rosemary Magee 1981PHD as the first female university secretary at Emory. When Magee stepped down nine years later to direct the Rose Library, Allison Dykes, the vice president for alumni relations, stepped in as vice president and secretary of the university.

2. After the admission of women as residential students in Emory College, in an era that now seems as distant in time and space as hoop skirts and parasols, the Quad served as the hunting ground for the annual Sadie Hawkins Day race. Male students would try to outrun coeds hot on their heels in a tradition prompted by the old comic strip

Li'l Abner. In the comic strip, young men captured by their pursuers in the race were required to marry them. In the Quad version, the men were pledged to take their captors on dates. Other runners of the Quad appeared in the 1970s—naked undergraduates who participated in the nationwide and thankfully brief fad of streaking.

3. John Stone, "The Spirits of This Lawn," in *Where Courageous Inquiry Leads*, ed. Hauk and Wolff King, 1–2.

4. The university in 1926 designated a fine arts center as one of the goals in the ten-year campaign to raise $10 million. Had the campaign succeeded, the center might now stand on the site of the current Administration Building. As the Great Depression dashed any hopes of building the center, the administration took an alternative path by building Glenn Memorial as both a worship space and a performance auditorium—a function the building filled well until the dedication of the Donna and Marvin Schwartz Center for Performing Arts in 2003.

Bibliography

Archives and Manuscript Collections

All archives and manuscript collections are located in the Stuart A. Rose Manuscript, Archives, and Rare Book Library unless otherwise noted.

Young John Allen Papers, 1854–1938.
Woolford Bales Baker Audio Recordings, 1982–1984.
Digital Collections, Special Collections and Archives, Georgia State University Library.
Asa Griggs Candler Papers, 1821–1951.
Emory College. Board of Trustees Records, 1837–1919.
Emory College General Records. Series 1, Events and Activities, 1814–1918. Arbor Day.
Emory College Photograph Collection, 1868–1898, undated. Oxford College Library of Emory University.
Emory Junior College at Valdosta Records, 1928–1953.
Emory University. Anniversary Observances Collection, 1936–2011.
Emory University. Biographical Files, circa 1880–1990.
Emory University. Board of Trustees Records, 1914–2010.
Emory University. Emory Environs Collection, 1928–1994.
Emory University. Office of Business Management. Buildings and Facilities Files, 1927–1993.
Emory University. Office of the Secretary, circa 1980–2000, and 1989–1990.
Emory University. Photograph Collection, 1860–2003.
Emory University Senate Records. Committee on the Environment. Murdy-Carter Report.
Georgia Conference Manual Labor School. Board of Trustees Minutes, 1835–1838.
Melvin H. Goodwin Papers, 1938–1991.

Alexander Means Papers, 1824–1963.

Oxford College Photograph Collection, 1906–2015, undated. Oxford College Library of Emory University.

Joseph A. and Aaronetta Pierce Papers, circa 1900–2012.

Jeanie and Arthur Tufts Family Papers, 1838–1970.

Other Sources

Abrams, Ann Uhry. *Formula for Fortune: How Asa Candler Discovered Coca-Cola and Turned It into the Wealth His Children Enjoyed.* Bloomington, Ind.: iUniverse, 2012.

Auslander, Mark. *The Accidental Slaveowner: Revisiting a Myth of Race and Finding an American Family.* Athens: University of Georgia Press, 2011.

Bullock, Henry Morton. *A History of Emory University.* Nashville, Tenn.: Parthenon Press, 1936.

Conklin, Paul Keith. *Gone with the Ivy: A Biography of Vanderbilt University.* Knoxville: University of Tennessee Press, 1985.

Cuttino, George Peddy. *Dooley's Book: A Guide to the Emory University Campus.* Atlanta, Ga.: Emory University, 1986.

Duke, Marshall P. "'Emory Are Here': Emory as Place and Story." In Hauk and Wolff King, *Where Courageous Inquiry Leads*, 3–12.

Emory College (website). "Reclaiming the Grandeur: Candler Library Renovation and Addition." http://college.emory.edu/program/candler /readingroom/.

Emory University. *The Emory Alumnus* (November 1958).

Emory University (website). History and Traditions. "Makers of History." http://www.emoryhistory.emory.edu/facts-figures/people /makers-history/.

English, Thomas H. *Emory University, 1915–1965: A Semicentennial History.* Atlanta, Ga.: Emory University, 1965.

Hauk, Gary S. *A Legacy of Heart and Mind: Emory since 1836.* Atlanta, Ga.: Emory University, 1999.

Hauk, Gary S. *Religion and Reason Joined: Candler at One Hundred.* Atlanta, Ga.: Emory University, Candler School of Theology, 2014.

Hauk, Gary S., and Sally Wolff King, eds. *Where Courageous Inquiry Leads: The Emerging Life of Emory University.* Atlanta, Ga.: Emory University, 2010.

Henry, Scott. "Razed in Atlanta: Six Great Buildings We Lost." *Atlanta Magazine*, February 14, 2017. http://www.atlantamagazine.com /news-culture-articles/razed-atlanta-6-great-buildings-lost/.

Hermes, Richard. "The Haunting of Uppergate House. *Emory Magazine*, Winter 2000. http://www.emory.edu/EMORY_MAGAZINE/ winter2000/uppergate.html.

King, Barry. "Few Pieces to Pick up after Emory Blaze." *Atlanta Constitution*, January 4, 1979.

Jacobs, Hal. "Oxford College President's House Gets a New Lease on Life." *Emory Magazine,* Spring 2014, http://news.emory.edu/stories/2014/05/emag_oxford_presidents_home/campus.html.

Knight, Lucian Lamar. *Georgia's Landmarks, Memorials, and Legends.* Atlanta, Ga.: Byrd, 1914.

Mann, Harold W. *Atticus Greene Haygood: Methodist Bishop, Editor, and Educator.* Athens: University of Georgia Press, 2010.

May, James W. *The Glenn Memorial Story: A Heritage in Trust, a History of the United Methodist Church on the Emory University Campus.* Atlanta, Ga.: Glenn Memorial United Methodist Church, 1985.

Moon, Joseph C. *An Uncommon Place: Oxford College of Emory University.* Rev. ed. Oxford, Ga.: Oxford College of Emory University, 2003–2014.

North, Arthur T. "Emory University, Atlanta, Georgia: Henry Hornbostel, Architect." *American Architect* 118, no. 2337 (October 6, 1920): 429–32.

Oliver, Erik Blackburn. *Cornerstone and Grove: A Portrait in Architecture and Landscape of Emory's Birthplace in Oxford, Georgia.* Oxford, Ga.: Oxford College of Emory University, 2009.

Oliver, Erik Blackburn. *Images of America: Oxford.* Charleston, S.C.: Arcadia, 2014.

Oxford Historical Society. "George Washington Whitfield Stone Sr." Accessed May 7, 2018. http://www.oxfordhistoricalsociety.org/gww-stone-sr.html.

Partin, Clyde, Sr. *Athletics for All: A History of Health, Physical Education, Athletics, and Recreation at Emory University, 1836–2005.* Edited by Gary S. Hauk. Atlanta, Ga.: Emory University/Lenz, 2006.

Sams, Richard H. "The Hardman Cemetery and Meeting House, the Shallowford Indian Trail, and the Houston Chapel." Unpublished paper. DeKalb, Georgia, History Center Archives.

Seideman, Nancy. "Lullwater and the Greening of Emory: Catalyst for a New Environmental Commitment." In Hauk and Wolff King, *Where Courageous Inquiry Leads*, 71–81.

Stone, John. "The Spirits of This Lawn." In Hauk and Wolff King, *Where Courageous Inquiry Leads*, 1–2.

Thomas, John D. "Enigma: A Ring around Oxford." *Emory Magazine,* Spring 1998. http://www.emory.edu/EMORY_MAGAZINE/spring98/enigmabell.html.

Index